THE SPEED GAME

THE SPEED GAME

MY FAST TIMES IN BASKETBALL

Paul Westhead

UNIVERSITY OF NEBRASKA PRESS   LINCOLN

Library of Congress Cataloging-in-Publication Data
Names: Westhead, Paul, 1939– author. |
University of Nebraska Press.
Title: The speed game: my fast times
in basketball / Paul Westhead.
Description: Lincoln: University of Nebraska Press, 2020.
Identifiers: LCCN 2020011828
ISBN 9781496222602 (Hardback: acid-free paper)
ISBN 9781496224057 (ePub)
ISBN 9781496224064 (mobi)
ISBN 9781496224071 (PDF)
Subjects: LCSH: Westhead, Paul, 1939– | Basketball
coaches—United States—Biography. |
Basketball—Coaching—United States.
Classification: LCC GV884.W46 A3 2020 |
DDC 796.323092 [B]—dc23
LC record available at https://lccn.loc.gov/2020011828

Set in Lyon by Laura Buis.
Designed by N. Putens.

CONTENTS

INTRODUCTION

I wrote this book at two different times in my life. The first time was the year after I coached the Los Angeles Lakers. We won an NBA championship in 1980, and then eighteen months later I was fired. Scott Ostler, a beat writer with the *Los Angeles Times*, covering the Lakers, once asked me, "Why did you insert your fast break system with a Laker team that had just won a world championship with a proven style of play? You had a new contract, and owner Jerry Buss proclaimed you were the best coach in the world. Why Paul, why mess with success?"

Well, the answer is in the stories about to unfold in the pages ahead, or maybe not. To be honest, twenty coaching jobs later, I'm still figuring out why I gave up a sure thing with the best players, the best owner, in the best city. In doing so, the fast break system put my family in harm's way, as I was constantly being fired and run out of town. With my special game, I promised to knock your socks off, but I frequently got run out on a rail, with my socks on and nothing else to show for my coaching.

Ostler's question implies that all I had to do was hold a pat hand and I would have won titles over and over. I would have been rich and famous. So, Paul, why did you discard success for speed? Early in my coaching career, I was bit by the fast break bug and could never get "the system" out of my system.

Once I discovered the running game, I couldn't go back to normal basketball. It seemed dull and unrewarding. The speed game was exciting and full of adventure. After coaching summers in Puerto Rico and spending time with coach Sonny Allen at SMU (Southern Methodist University), I became the poster child for fast break basketball. Some said that I was attempting to destroy the game, but really, I was attempting to push the envelope to more and more scoring, to *better* basketball.

I resumed writing about my coaching after my time at Loyola Marymount University. My team had averaged 122 points per game and went to the Elite Eight in the 1990 NCAA tournament, in one of the most magical runs ever seen.

We were a high-wire act capable of flying past opponents. No team in the United States played like us; we lured you into our pace of play and then watched you crumble in exhaustion. My LMU (Loyola Marymount University) team ran the fast break system to perfection. After twenty years of experimentation, I finally mastered the system. Full-court offense and shoot the ball in five seconds and then press defensively full court and make the opponent shoot the ball in five seconds—the speed game was complete. The trap was set. Opponents were caught in our running game.

My 1990 LMU team was going to show the world the fast break was king. We had the leading scorer and rebounder in the NCAA with Hank Gathers. In the running game, Hank was unstoppable. He could score and rebound offensively at will. Hank was complemented by Bo Kimble, his former high school teammate who could score as well as Hank. Together, they were unbeatable. Kimble excelled at shooting long outside jumpers, and Gathers attacked the basket, scoring inside. The stage was set. We were going to knock your socks off. Then, during the conference tournament, tragedy struck. Hank Gathers collapsed on the basketball court and died.

That moment changed me and my team forever. Our team continued to play in the NCAA tournament. We won games without our fallen hero, Hank Gathers. Actually, we won games for Hank Gathers. The team wanted to do it for Hank. Even the returning NCAA champions, University of Michigan, could not stop the speed game. The outcome was sealed; victory was ours.

With success in hand, as when I won the NBA championship with the Los Angeles Lakers, I left LMU.

Dale Brown, coach of Louisiana State University, said to me, "Why did you leave college coaching? Your fast break style was about to change the way basketball was played. Paul, you were about to create a new way, and you departed back to the NBA. Why?"

Always the question: Why Paul?

To follow my system of basketball, I had to be a genius who saw the game as a work of art . . . or an uninformed person who followed a stupid path. The former NBA coach Alex Hannum called my system "crapadoodle." Who in their right mind would demand players to sprint on every offensive possession and then defend full court on every defensive possession? It smacks of madness or, more accurately, stupidity.

What kind of coach would avoid practicing defending ball screens in the half court because you will never be defending in the half court? What coach would avoid practicing offensive play sets because your team was going to run fast break every possession and not need any play calls? This sounds downright irresponsible as a coach: "Stupid, stupid, stupid."

And yet there is a stroke of genius in the scheme of press and run, press and run the entire game. The pace of the game will wear out the opponent no matter how superior in talent. The opposition will falter against the speed if it is nonstop. The genius is in eliminating all the ordinary things players do to slow the game down. Give them no option except to play the speed game.

If your team has play sets on offense, then the players will do them and not run fast break. So genius says eliminate play sets and only run offense as fast as you can. The risk is if your players slow down, they need play sets, and without plays, your team will look disorganized and lose.

The coach will look stupid and get fired. The fast break system is all or nothing. When the players buy into the speed game, it is art in motion. It is genius. When they don't buy in, usually because it is too hard, it is chaos. It is stupid.

In my coaching career, I chose to walk the fine line between genius and stupid. Most of my coaching jobs, I looked stupid. But every once in a while, like at LMU with Hank Gathers and Bo Kimble, I looked like a genius. The risk was worth the fleeting moment of pure speed.

Hopefully the pages ahead will shed some light on why I started the fast break with the Lakers and lost my job because of it and then why I left the speed game at LMU when it was going full throttle.

The questions by Scott Ostler and Dale Brown are a contradiction. Perhaps, my coaching career of twenty jobs is a continual conflict.

As the poet Walt Whitman said, "Do I contradict myself? Very well, then I contradict myself; I am large, I contain multitudes." Well, I am no creative genius like Walt Whitman, but I am stubborn. Here's hoping the chapters ahead will redeem me.

I hope I knock your socks off.

THE SPEED GAME

1

West Philly

We came into the world like brother and brother, / And now let's go hand in hand, not one before another.

—WILLIAM SHAKESPEARE, *Comedy of Errors*

My parents, Cy and Jane, were part of the post–World War II working middle class—Monday through Friday, nine to five, make enough to pay the bills and then go back to work again Monday morning and start all over again.

As a young boy in grammar school, I was raised in a row house in West Philadelphia, where your neighbors were a thin wall away from your living room on either side. In the winter, the house was freezing; in the summer, it was so hot that everyone sat outside on the steps.

As a kid, I played sports with the neighborhood gang, never on an organized team with uniforms and a real coach. In my neighborhood there were no Saturday morning Little League games. We made up a team and played with whoever came around that day.

All our games were contained on the street. We played half ball with a broomstick and a rubber ball cut in half. The pitcher would sail the ball, and the batter would attempt to tag it with the stick. If you caught the floating half ball just right, it would glide fifty feet in the air over the pitcher for a home run.

To get a swing, you sat on the curb and waited your turn. Smart kids would bring their dinner outside to get ahead of others. However, if you came outside with food and didn't say, "No hunks, no nothing!" you would have your dinner taken away and devoured by the gang. Those were the rules, and everybody knew the rules.

I still remember running out to play, with a meatball sandwich, and having it taken away by older kids who chanted, "You didn't say, 'No hunks!'" In fact, the memory and the trauma of that is so ingrained that, to this day, when I have a meatball sandwich, I picture street thugs grabbing my food from me.

My parents never saw me play much, because our made-up games were during their work hours. My father would occasionally show up to check us out, while my mom would be home cleaning the house and cooking. They took good care of us two boys, but sports were not in the mix.

I remember being led around by my older brother, Pete, as a young three-year-old. Both of my parents worked all week, so Pete was in charge. He took me to St. Monica's preschool and made sure I was fed by the nuns at lunch. He dragged me to the playground after school with his eight-year-old buddies. One day, Pete said, "We're leaving," and we stormed out of our grandparents' house on Eighteenth Street in South Philadelphia to seek greener pastures at our other grandmother's home in West Philadelphia. I had no idea of the dispute, but my brother, Pete, said, "Let's go." He was my leader, so willingly I ran away with Pete.

The night before my first day of school, my mom gave me and Pete a bath together. Normally, we got a bath once a week on Saturday night, but this was special. In fact, I was so concerned about not being late for school the next day that I got dressed in my pants, shirt, and tie before bed. I carefully lay down and didn't move the whole night. At 6:00 a.m. I popped up, ran down to breakfast, and was ready to go, inside of ten minutes. We had an eight-block walk to school, and I wasn't going to be late.

The school day became a blur as I blended in with ninety other first-grade boys just like me. It was more like prison: sit down, stand up, raise your hand, and say, "Sister, may I?" My brother, Pete, was in fifth grade and so was more relaxed about school. Frequently, after my mom made our lunch and then left for work as a switchboard operator, Pete would declare that he was sick and not going to school. He was the boss, so I had to stay home also. A half hour later Pete would declare that it was lunchtime, and we would sit and eat Mom's prepared school sandwiches. Oftentimes, Pete would eat my lunch too.

My six years at Most Blessed Sacrament School and the streets of West Philadelphia taught me to take care of myself. If you wanted something in life, you had to do it yourself.

My brother became my guardian angel. It was Pete who brought me into the gang on the corner. Pete had a winning way with his peers despite not being a good athlete. When my brother was three, he contracted polio— they called it infantile paralysis back then—after swimming at the seashore. When he was a teenager, they performed major surgery on Pete's legs, shoulders, and arms, and then he had to do all kinds of rehab. He was in the Shriners Hospital for almost a year.

After that, he could walk and do things, but he couldn't run and jump, like the other kids in the neighborhood. When he played games like basketball, he was very limited. Falling was the worst thing that could happen to him, because he couldn't put his hands down to brace himself, and once he was down, he would not be able to get up.

Still, I don't remember my mom ever saying, "Poor Pete." In fact, I don't remember her ever sharing any frustration about her firstborn having polio. Both my mom and my brother got pretty raw deals as kids, and yet neither of them were whiners or complainers. They just kind of got on with it.

I think that's why the neighbor kids liked Pete, because he tried. He could have easily been a kid who just sat in the bleachers and cried, but instead he said, "No, I want to be out there." They respected that. He had a sharp wit; he was a smart guy. After the game, he was really one of the guys. He won them over by his presence, not by his performance, and then by his smarts and his charm. And he had me to run and jump for him.

You see, as it turns out, my brother, Pete, was a coach; he was *my* coach. I was a player, maybe not a very good one, but we were stuck with each other, sometimes literally. When the corner gang would play pickup baseball, Pete would be selected late in the draw with me at his side. The opposing team allowed Pete to bat and me to stand next to him and run. We were a good combination. Pete would get wood on the pitch, and I would run like hell to first base. I couldn't hit, but I was fast. I now realize this was the start of my athletic career.

As a seven-year-old, I was competing with older boys who still treated me as their peer. Frequently, I was shoved around and lost the battle, but a determination to keep going was building up inside me. I had no choice—Pete was always at my side, and with Pete, there was no backing down.

One time, while playing street baseball, the ball was hit into the sewer. Because I was the youngest and the smallest, I was grabbed and lowered into the sewer headfirst. With my hands in the black muck, I found the ball, as well as a few others from previous games. The older guys then wanted to have some fun with me and lower me deeper into the sewer to dunk my head in the muck. Fortunately for me, Pete was there telling the guys, "Enough, bring him up street level," and they did.

Even though he couldn't do athletic things, Pete drilled me on how to catch a football, hit a fastball, and most importantly, shoot a basketball. My first attempt to play basketball was on a wide street at Fifty-Fourth and Warrington Avenue. It was a few blocks from home, but there was a peach basket—yes, an actual peach basket—nailed to a telephone pole to shoot hoops. At age ten, I was not able to shoot smoothly to the ten-foot basket. I had to launch it like a shot-putter. On one occasion, I stepped back to take a twenty-foot shot, and a car ran over my foot. The car squashed the back of my sneaker, and I was frozen. The car didn't move, and I couldn't move. The shot slammed against the telephone pole, and the ball rolled down the street. Finally, the car moved forward, and my foot was free. Lucky for me, there was "no harm, no foul." I went home with no broken bones but was convinced basketball was not for me.

Of course, what I believed wasn't important. Pete wanted me to play basketball, so as a ten-year-old, I was taught basketball in our West Philadelphia row house bathroom. We cut out a shoebox and nailed it above the doorjamb. Pete demanded that I shoot a tennis ball and follow through over and over. He didn't allow careless releases. If I was playing baseball and got a single, he'd say, "If you hustled, you probably could have gotten a double." He was always looking for better from me, always demanding perfection on every shot attempt. Sometimes I resented how he pushed me, but years later, as a basketball coach, I demanded the same release and same perfection from NBA players.

And even then, well into my professional coaching career, he was still coaching me. He was very opinionated and would call me and say, "Why'd you play that guy, he can't play dead!"

When I moved from Philadelphia to Los Angeles to coach the Lakers, I missed the daily interaction with Pete. Gone was my brother telling me how to attack Temple University's zone defense. Gone was Pete saying, "Throw the lob pass to Jim Crawford," at La Salle. "Trust me. Crawford is a great leaper; he will catch and score." Once I moved to LA, I didn't have my brother whispering in my ear.

For the next thirty-five years, I called my brother, Pete, every day at his home in New Jersey. He always had coaching advice on my team. "Get the ball to Kareem in the low post, and play Michael Cooper on Larry Bird. He is your best defender." Pete's words were not always kind to my coaching decisions. He was critical, but he cared. Pete felt as though if my team lost, he lost.

I don't know if I idolized my brother, but I respected him, and I loved him. And while he was my guardian angel, it didn't prevent him from hustling me now and then. As kids in our row house, we shared one bedroom with twin beds and one window. We were sweltering in the summer and freezing in the winter. I can still remember the day Pete said in all sincerity, "You know, we should switch beds every six months just to be fair." That sounded reasonable to me, so I agreed. It took me a long time to figure what Pete had done—he ended up every summer with the cooler bed by the window and every winter with the warmer bed by the wall.

Pete was pretty clever.

WE MOVED FROM West Philadelphia to Lansdowne, Pennsylvania, when I was in seventh grade. I was trying to find something to impress my new schoolmates, to show I was tough, to show I could handle myself. My parish school, St. Philomena's, had a boxing team, so I joined. I was five feet, seventy-five pounds, and wanting to grow up. On Wednesday nights, we practiced in the school basement. One-on-one duels usually ended with a bloody nose or dizziness from a headbutt. One kid, Sam, was bigger and stronger than all the other fighters. When Coach Bob assigned Sam to me, I knew I was going down. It was a good lesson to get knocked off your feet. As Vince Lombardi said, "It's not whether you get knocked down; it's whether you get back up." And Sam knocked me down.

After ten months of practice, we had a boxing match in Chester, Pennsylvania. This was in a real arena, in a real ring, and against a real opponent who didn't know or like you. The fight was three one-minute rounds with sixteen-ounce gloves. You can't imagine how long sixty seconds can be in a ring with someone trying to knock you out. It's longer than an entire math class. In the middle of round two, I headbutted my opponent and then had my way with him. It wasn't an intentional hit, but it was effective. I was declared the winner. Having my arm raised by the judge made me want more moments of victory, and I got the taste of winning. Boxing taught me to overcome the enemy. I had the same feeling playing, and later coaching, basketball.

LANSDOWNE IS A suburb about five miles outside Philadelphia. I went to a very small Catholic grade school, maybe fifteen kids in a class. I liked Lansdowne—it didn't mean anything to me to move. I mean, it wasn't like I had everything going for me in Philly.

Still, when it came time for high school, my parents sent me back into the city to attend West Catholic High School. To get there and back, I had to hitchhike to and from West Philadelphia every day. It taught me to be clever in things I never had to be clever at before. You see, going to school was an easy hitchhike, because there weren't a lot of kids from Lansdowne going into the city, so there wasn't a lot of competition for rides.

It was in coming home where you had all the competition, because all the kids were getting out at the same time. I remember that the school was at Forty-Ninth and Chestnut. Chestnut was a one-way street coming into the city; Walnut was one way going out. If you stood at Forty-Ninth, there would already be twenty kids there, competing for rides. If you went down to Forty-Eighth, it was fifteen kids, and there would be another ten at Forty-Seventh. But if you walked down to Forty-Fourth Street, it was just you and a couple of buddies.

That was trick one. Trick number two was to have your thumb out so that a guy would stop. And when you'd say, "Hey, can you give me a ride?" he'd say, "Sure kid, get on in," and open his door. Then four of your buddies would rush in the car with you. He wouldn't have let you in if he had known they were coming.

My first attempt to play on a real basketball team was at West Catholic. I went out for the freshman team along with one hundred other boys and was cut. My parents encouraged me to continue practicing basketball even if that meant not getting a job to help our financial situation.

My mom had been born and raised in South Philadelphia, and after fourth grade she was pulled out of school and went to work for the family. Her family, the Carneys, had twelve kids, so this was a big operation. Somebody had to go shopping every day. Because she was quick and fast and enterprising, they picked her out. One day, my grandfather said, "Jane, you're going to be with me," and that was the end of her schooling.

My mom was a very smart person, but according to the standards of education, she never got past the fourth grade. And I think that's why my mom never pushed me to work the way she was pushed to work. I'm sure it was her way of saying that what happened to her wasn't going to happen to her son. Jane was determined that her sons were going to pursue their dreams and not be cut short because of money. Her life's mission was her boys. She lived for her sons.

Because of that, she worried about us a lot. She worried that I was undernourished because I really didn't like a lot of foods as a kid. Pete, on the other hand, loved everything, including anything I was eating, which he helped himself to quite often. I remember that my mom had become so concerned about me once that she made two chickens for dinner: one for the family and one just for me. Pete helped me out with that too.

2

Stretching

After many hours of basketball drills, directed by Pete watching me, I went out for the varsity basketball team at West Catholic again in tenth grade. I was a skinny, five-foot-two kid who didn't have a chance against bigger city players. For the second time, I was cut. In my third year, I was cut once more.

Although I was disappointed, I wasn't in any way embarrassed. You have to understand, there was no shame in being cut at West Catholic. It was a powerhouse team, an all-boys school of more than 2,500. If you didn't make the team, you played for your homeroom. They had a homeroom basketball league, and at the end of the season, they would declare a homeroom champion. On one occasion, the homeroom champs beat the varsity in a scrimmage; that's how close the competition was. There were a lot of kids at West Catholic who got scholarships only playing for their homerooms.

Before my last try to make the varsity, Pete came up with a new plan. Somehow, I was going to grow from five feet two to six feet two in a year. Every night before bed, Pete would stretch my legs over and over, taking one leg and pulling it while I held on to something and then using the same method on the other leg. This would last for ten minutes. Pete called it "stretching"; it was, more accurately, "pulling" or, most accurately, "torture." When this was done, he would have me hang by my arms on the doorjamb to stretch my upper body. It was uncomfortable, but believe it or not, I actually ended up growing a foot in a year. Did Pete's stretches have anything to do with it? I have no idea.

MY HIGH SCHOOL summers were spent at the outdoor courts next to Lansdowne High School. I would go in the morning and shoot baskets before the other players would arrive. Many times, the early arrivals would play cards until enough guys showed up. You see, in the neighborhood, being good at basketball was the number one thing for establishing yourself in the pecking order. Being good at playing cards was second. I was good at poker and frequently won a few dollars before the basketball games started. Most of the regular card game players were from the basketball team at Lansdowne High.

I was the outcast, a kid from a Catholic school who didn't make his high school team. Because of this stigma, I had to wait around to be selected. Once in, however, it was all about how you played. The law of the jungle was winners stay and losers sit, so you could play for ten minutes and then sit for two hours or win and keep playing for two hours. Local Lansdowne stars like Lou Bayne and Drew and Art Hyland accepted me into the pack. My hero was Jim Brangan, a terrific shooter who helped me with my game. When I was on Jim's team, I did anything to win and stay with him.

I was free to play basketball because my parents, mainly my mom, didn't force me to get a job. I think she felt if I was free in the summer, it would help my development as a basketball player. Still, I did work. For a while, I worked as a caddy at Llanerch Country Club, about five miles from our home.

Now, these days, even at nice private courses like Riviera, not a lot of people use caddies, but back then everybody did. To caddy, you'd get to the course around eight in the morning and sit around the caddy shack with about one hundred other people. The caddy master would call the grown men first, there were about twenty-five of them. And it was their full-time job, so there were no hard feelings about them being called first.

But after that, it was all about whom the caddy master knew from a friend of a friend, or maybe he needed to help out the son of a member, stuff like that. Being called then depended a lot on who you knew. And I didn't know anybody. Some days it would get to be 3:30 in the afternoon, and the caddy master would say, "Okay, that's it for today," and I wouldn't have gotten anything. Even worse, sometimes you'd get called at 3:15 p.m. You'd been sitting for six hours, and now you were going to be out for another five hours, which meant you wouldn't get in until way after 8:00 p.m.

You got paid two dollars a bag, and sometimes you got paid double for carrying two bags. At the end, they'd give you four dollars, and if they thought you did a good job, they'd each give you fifty cents. So on a good day, you'd make five bucks.

I started to discover that things were better when I didn't get called, because after all the men got called out, it was just the kids about ages fourteen to twenty-four, and we'd play cards while we waited. On days like that, sometimes I'd win ten or fifteen bucks just playing cards. When I'd get home, my mom would ask how I did, and I'd say, "Good round today, Mom. *Very* good round."

SUMMERS IN LANSDOWNE gave me the confidence to play basketball in college. Even though I never made my high school team, I could thrive with guys who were good high school players. And if my plan to play college basketball didn't work, the summers at least taught me to be a card shark. I now look back and wonder why I spent so much time on basketball. The answer is I had nothing else. If I had walked out of the house with a tennis racket and shorts, the neighborhood kids would have beaten me up and sent me home. My way out of this dull, uneventful life was through basketball. If I failed, I was destined for a life of Thursday night bowling on the Ricky's Bar and Grill squad. In Philadelphia, everybody was to do the same things from birth to death. Don't rock the boat. Basketball was my chance to rock the boat and do something new and exciting.

When I was sixteen, I began playing in a bar league with the Kiligian Roofers, a group of thirty-five-year-olds who let me join my first team. There was a guy named Eddie Snow who was older, like thirty-six, and he played in the summers in Lansdowne. He was a nice guy who could really shoot the ball. He took a liking to me, and when I got cut from the West Catholic team, he found out and said, "Why don't you come play with us?"

I never actually played in games with them, because I was too young and inexperienced; they were old and needed the minutes to reduce their beer bellies. After the games, when the players would go to the tavern for drinks and laughs, I would go home for math problems and stretching, always the stretching, which, kind of incredibly, paid off, because by my senior year at West Catholic, I had grown to exactly the six feet two Pete had mandated.

So I felt good going into my final tryout at West Catholic, and it went well. I made the first ten days of practice and believed I needed just one more good performance to make the team. Tryouts were brutal. Two hundred guys would try out, and of them, fifty were good enough to make the team. Every day, you knew if you would be allowed back to the next practice, because a list would appear on the locker room door with the names of all those who made it from the previous day.

Though I had always made it until day eight or nine, this time I made it all the way until the final day, so I felt good about my chances. I felt even better when the coach, Jim Usilton, came over and told me, "You're good enough to play on my team." But that was the end of the good times, because he followed up by saying, "But you don't have any experience, and as a senior, I have to let you go."

Cut again.

Again, there was no shame in getting cut. No shame because you knew you weren't the only one; there were a lot of good guys who didn't make it. There were at least another fifteen guys like me who could have made the team. Still, getting cut again meant my future after high school graduation seemed to have been reduced to college night classes while riding the bench for the Kiligian Roofers.

I DON'T KNOW how it evolved, the idea of me going to a prep school after high school. I guess my parents saw me looking through some magazines that advertised those schools, which were mostly in the South and seemed like a world away. But they also offered the opportunity for me to finally play high school basketball.

My friend Jim Brangan had gone to Lawrenceville Prep after high school and then to Princeton University, where he became captain of the basketball team. Much of my interest in prep school was because of Brangan. He was a star player and needed prep school. I was a nobody and surely needed prep school. If Jim Brangan could do it, there was hope for me.

I found a local school, Malvern Prep, run by the Augustinian Fathers and connected to Villanova. I would be able to play as a fifth-year student at Malvern since I never played at West Catholic; that was the one benefit of having been cut all those years, I maintained all my athletic eligibility.

The hitch was that Malvern cost $3,000 per year back then, and my parents didn't have $30 to spend. My dream to finally play basketball seemed to be dissolving. My parents, however, decided to take out a bank loan for $3,000 to give me a chance to play. This was a significant risk for my parents, and I'm sure it was driven by my mother. My father was a salesman, and he would deal in hypotheticals, you know: "Maybe we should take out a loan to get Paul into Malvern." My mom would say, "Yeah, we're going to send him to Malvern, and I'm going to pay for it."

They had to go to the bank and work this out. It wasn't as if they could use a credit card; $3,000 at this time would buy you a house.

The thing was, once I got in, I do remember I absolutely hated it. I absolutely hated Malvern. I was a postgraduate student, a fifth-year senior, at an exclusive school with a bunch of rich kids. It would be someone's birthday, and they would drive up in a convertible and say, "Look at what my parents got me." They had no need or time for me or had anything in common with me. It was the loneliest I've ever felt.

I took the school bus to Malvern. I'd never taken a bus to West Catholic. The bus didn't leave Malvern until 5:00 p.m. each day, so from 2:30 until 5:00, there was nothing for me to do except just sit around. I came home day one or day two, and I told my mom I didn't like it. I knew my mom would understand. She didn't give me the "Well, we paid a lot of money" speech. She said, "Okay, just give it another week. And then we'll talk about it."

The following week, I met some guys. One of them, Upton Bell, was the son of Bert Bell, the commissioner of the NFL. As it turned out, he was a basketball player like me and a fifth-year senior. So I hung in another week. And the next thing you know, I started playing basketball, and I was home free.

Still, I was way out of my league. The only thing I had that made me feel kind of accepted was basketball. And even with that, I always felt as though there were kids on the team who felt I was I was imposing. I mean, here I show up, and I'm the leading scorer on the team—a guy who had been playing with roofers was the leading scorer in the league. I did well, but I can see where there would be some degree of hard feelings.

Still, looking back, this was the tipping point of my playing career. I went to Malvern and became the leading scorer in the Inter-Academic League. Because of that, I got a tryout with St. Joseph's College. Thanks to Jane and Cy's sacrifice, and gamble, I became a player.

COACH JACK RAMSAY of St. Joseph's had heard of me through one of his players, Jack Savage, who grew up in my neighborhood in West Philadelphia. Savage kept asking Ramsay, "Have you seen the Westhead kid play?" Ramsay said he hadn't gotten around to it, but he told Savage to tell me to come to campus and play with Jack and his buddies and he would watch.

A week before the scheduled visit, I hurt my ankle in a pickup game on the playground. It was so swollen I couldn't walk for three days. I kept putting it in hot water, and it kept getting more swollen. (What a dummy.) I should have canceled my tryout at St. Joe's, but I knew there would never be another chance. After being cut four years in a row, I was going to show up.

We played three-on-three, half court. I was known for my ability to muscle my way to the rim and score on driving lay-ups, but because of my injured ankle, I was forced to shoot outside, two-hand set shots. Miraculously, I made 25 of 30 attempts. Afterward, Jack Ramsay said he might have a scholarship for me, believing he had found the outside shooter his team desperately needed.

Four years later at a team dinner, Jack said to me, "Paul, you made more outside shots in that pickup game than you did in four years with our team." The look on his face told me I pulled one over on him. But it was okay; he liked my four years with him. Even though I wasn't a star player, I was a student athlete. My academic grade point average of 3.4 was higher than my 2.4 points per game average. That was acceptable for Dr. Jack Ramsay.

3

Jersey Girl

Upon graduating from St. Joseph's College in 1961, I was done playing basketball. I wasn't good enough for professional ball, and the neighborhood beer league had no appeal. I received a fellowship to Villanova University to study English literature for the next two years; I was a scholar focused on William Shakespeare.

I enjoyed my life as a scholar. Six hours a day doing research in the library was more satisfying than practicing my jump shot on the basketball court. Plus, I was better at quoting Hamlet than shooting.

In September of my second year at Villanova, a buddy and I decided to go watch the Phillies play. The game got rained out, so we decided to go downtown and headed into a bar where we saw two young women sitting at a table. One of them was a Jersey girl named Cassie Molloy.

My buddy walked over and did all the talking, eventually asking them if they'd like to have a drink with us. I was a twenty-one-year-old kid who had been pretty much of a dud with the ladies. There was no fast break in this part of my game. My buddy Joe Keel, on the other hand, was pretty good. So we sat down and talked, Joe handling the majority of those duties. Eventually, we escorted them home and made plans to all attend a Villanova football game the following day.

We met in downtown pub. I walked in to find them sitting at a table with two other women, so I gave a little wave, because I was too scared to go sit with them without Joe there to carry the load. As it turned out, Joe was in the bathroom, so I got him and said, "Joe, they brought their mothers! What are we gonna do?" He said, "What are you talking about? Those are just some women sitting next to them, you idiot."

As I said, no game.

Still, that was September, and somehow, someway by Christmas Cassie and I were engaged. By February we were married. I guess you'd call it a whirlwind romance, though Cassie's mom always changed one fact: she told people we met on a blind date, because she didn't want people to know we'd actually met in a bar.

I was married, and I needed a job. I applied to Cheltenham High School as an English teacher. They also needed a varsity basketball coach. I interviewed for both. As a teacher, they welcomed me with open arms. As a coach, they said, "No thanks." I had no experience, no reputation, no game. To me, it was like getting cut from the basketball team at West Catholic High School all over again. I was angry with their decision, and so in a fit of pique, I also turned down the teaching offer.

But this was the spark that drove me into coaching basketball. I guess I'd finally had enough rejection from basketball; now I was going to show everyone what they missed out on. Now I wanted to do both: teach and coach.

I went to Jack Ramsay and asked if he would help me get an assistant basketball position at Widener College in Chester, Pennsylvania. He said he would make a call on my behalf but counseled, "Paul, you are a teacher, not a coach." In a polite way, he was telling me my future was not coaching basketball. Some of his former players such as Jack McKinney, Jim Lynam, and Matty Guokas were naturals for the game. I was not of their caliber. Coach Ramsay saw me as an academic, not a leader in basketball.

Truth be told, Ramsay was right. I had not grown up dreaming of being a coach. As a high school kid growing up, I had no aspirations of coaching— probably the opposite. Since I didn't make any team as a kid, I thought coaches were not of the highest level. High school was full of failure and disappointment when it came to basketball, so I didn't really admire the coach there. He obviously didn't admire me. I did catch a momentary break at Malvern Prep with my coach Dr. Gene Powers, who arrived the same year as me. That got me to St. Joe's, where I didn't get a lot of love once I arrived. Though I rose through the ranks each season, my senior year was pretty much destroyed by me breaking my wrist and missing three quarters of the season.

So if normal aspirations for being a coach are that you admire yours and he shows you how he directs people, that wasn't how it was for me. It was more like me being the guy at the end of the bench saying, "Man, this is a lot of bullshit."

I didn't get the job at Widener and moved on to my only offer, a teaching position at the University of Dayton. A professor at Villanova, Dr. B. J. Bedard, accepted an offer to teach at Dayton and asked me to come with him. I was now a married man with five classes of freshman English and hundreds of papers to grade each week.

To keep the coaching dream alive, I asked Jack Ramsay once again to call on my behalf, this time to Dayton. They said, "Thanks, but we are full." But soon after, Tom Blackburn, Dayton's head basketball coach, learned he had throat cancer and wouldn't be able to handle his duties. His new assistant Don Donoher would be taking over. Because of Jack Ramsay's call about me, Donoher came to me and asked if I would coach the freshman team. Suddenly, I was a college basketball coach. I finally made the team.

My first season with the Dayton Flyers, my team went 17-2-3; that's right, we had three ties. We had three ties because Coach Blackburn had a rule that the freshman games at Dayton must end by 7:00 p.m. sharp so that the varsity could enter. So on three occasions, at precisely 7:00 p.m., the score was even, the buzzer sounded, and both teams were escorted off the court. I might be the only basketball coach in history with three tie games on record.

Tom Blackburn passed away at the end of the season, and Don Donoher was named the new head coach. Me? I was once again cut and looking for a teaching-coaching position. As luck would have it, Cheltenham High School called and said they'd love to have me as an English teacher as well as their new basketball coach. Now that I had college coaching experience,

I was suddenly desirable. Cassie and I and our new baby girl, Monica, went back to Pennsylvania for my first true teaching-coaching position.

BEING A HIGH school teacher and basketball coach was one of the happiest periods of my career. I enjoyed discussing American literature with eager students who wanted to hear about Huck Finn, Captain Ahab, and Holden Caulfield. I also taught writing at Montgomery County Community College's night school once a week, because the head of the English department there had taught me at St. Joe's. And the prophecy had been fulfilled: Paul Westhead ended up at night school.

And I loved it.

Coaching, however, was more of a challenge. The team was accustomed to losing; Cheltenham had gone 2-18 the previous season. I was eager to change that, so my first year as coach, before I had ever run a single practice at Cheltenham, I attended a coaching clinic put on by Bobby Knight, then the coach at Army. I went up to West Point and watched his day-long clinic, full of drills and routines, 80 percent of which were defensive, and one of those drills began by putting one player at the top of one key and another at the top of the other and then rolling the ball out at half court and having the two players run to see who could get the ball first. Whoever won the ball was on offense, and the other was on defense.

Impressed, I decided to make this the first drill of my first practice. I had the first two boys come out, I rolled out the ball, and the two kids went after it at half court, crashing into each other. The star player from the previous season, Joe Dratch, stayed on the ground. It turned out he had a broken collarbone.

The *first* practice, the first *drill* of the first practice—it was not an auspicious start.

I was the classic hard-ass, do-it-by-the-book coach. I was Ramsay and then some. I was Bobby Knight: defense, toughness, and diving on the floor. Don't show any freedom to your players; just keep demanding more hard work. I was more than happy to win a game 55–53 and had no concept of the fast break.

A group from Ogontz Junior High arrived with a winning record and high expectations. In a few seasons, we turned things around, going from losing to powerhouse Chester High by 50 points to beating them in the playoffs by 25. Rich kids from the suburbs were beating kids from the inner city. I was coaching like I played; Jack Ramsay would be proud: tough man-to-man defense and controlled half-court offense.

I became a coach at Cheltenham High. I learned how to deal with people, how to be around players, how to deal with situations. In my first year, I met a kid named George Barton. He was a football player who showed signs that he might play basketball in the winter. I met with George, and he said, "Yes, after football, I will come out for your team." But he said he needed Saturday's free to work. His mother, a single mom, needed the money, and because of football, he hadn't worked for months.

As a brand-new coach, my rules allowed for no exception. Our team was going to practice on Saturdays, and I would tolerate no excuse. I never felt good about it. I felt as though I was doing the right thing only because I was a first-year coach who thought that if you have five rules, they never get broken. With ten years of experience and the same situation, I would have handled it differently.

George went home to talk to his mom. I went home hoping our strongest, most physical player would find a way. I wanted to tell George, "It's okay for you to miss Saturdays and help your mom," but I didn't. To my surprise, George Barton came to me and said, "I will be at every practice," and walked away.

That same week, I was on cafeteria duty, in charge of dealing with five hundred hungry students. A veteran teacher, Joe Newman, cautioned me that it was grapes and radish day. All five hundred food trays had cups of grapes and radishes. He said the students liked to throw them at each other. I was standing and watching when one went whizzing by my ear and went splat against the wall.

I looked out, and everyone was looking at me. A table of football players were laughing and pointing to the culprit, Richard Gold, and I yelled, "Richard Gold, come up here!" He grinned as if to say, "Come make me." Unexpectedly, I had a moment of truth: Do I storm down there and pull Richard Gold up to the front? Do I back off and act as if there was no harm, no foul? After all, I wasn't directly hit. All five hundred students were waiting for my response. Like a good baseball umpire with a close call at home plate, I paused to signal safe or out.

Just then, George Barton appeared behind Richard Gold and said, "The man called you up to him." George placed his powerful hands on Gold's collar and lifted him up out of his chair. Richard Gold, a defeated hero, came running up to me, sniveling and saying, "I'm sorry. I will clean it up." I was saved by my player, George Barton. It was the first of many times when one of my players solved a problem for the coach. Looking back, this was a tipping point in my coaching career. Without George's intervention, I would have been in the middle of an ugly situation, and my coaching credibility would have dropped.

Later that season, needing a defensive rebound to defeat our archrival, Abington High, George Barton went up and pulled the ball down to his chest, nearly squeezing the air out of it. It reminded me of the flying grape that whizzed by my ear; George saved me then and saved me again against Abington High. I honestly believe that without George Barton, I would never have made it to the Los Angeles Lakers.

4

Simplicity, Simplicity, Simplicity!

At Cheltenham, I followed the proven formula for Philadelphia basketball, and with my new players, it worked. The boys from Ogontz—Chuck Shectman, Rich Raden, Billy Half, and Craig Littlepage—did the rest. We went 26-0 and on to the state finals in Pittsburgh against the Western Pennsylvania champions. We were one shot away from victory, with eight seconds remaining, when our star center, Littlepage, took a turnaround hook shot, like Kareem Abdul-Jabbar, and it rimmed around and around and finally fell out. We ended up losing in overtime, but the thrill of our season remained. Not only did I love my players, but suddenly, quite unexpectedly, I was hooked on coaching, though not the kind of coaching I would become famous for.

In fact, of all the teams I have ever coached—and there have been a lot—the only one that ever asked me back for a reunion was the Cheltenham team. It was like thirty years later, and I found them sitting around having a beer and telling stories. Listening to them talk about their coach, I found myself thinking, "Is this me they're talking about?" They said, "Coach, you were such a hard-ass. We'd have a three-hour practice, and we'd be sitting in the hallway waiting for our parents to pick us up. And you'd walk by and refuse to look at us."

Funny thing was that I wasn't much older than them. They were eighteen; I was twenty-four. I loved teaching Robert Frost poetry, but I wanted more. As would become the norm in my life, it was Jack McKinney who offered me a new opportunity, this one to become his assistant coach at St. Joseph's College.

Though it was something I wanted, the decision to take it was by no means an easy one. I enjoyed teaching, and the Cheltenham community had really taken to my team, even painting the street signs our school colors. It would have been a perfect time to stay and build a program that I could have run until retirement.

The thing about Cheltenham, and later LMU, was that I had done it. I had not only won but also established something that was my own. Looking back at both situations, perhaps I should have stayed.

When I went to Cassie with the idea of going to St. Joseph's, she was supportive, which is how she's been throughout my professional life. Pretty much every step of the way, she's been the one to say, "Okay, let's try it."

I did, and we were off to St. Joe's. As a college coach, I had two main duties: helping to coach the team and going to high school games in Philadelphia to check out talent. This is back in the day when there was one head coach and one assistant. That was it. We did everything.

THE WESTHEADS AND the McKinneys didn't live far apart from each other in the Drexel Hill neighborhood of Philadelphia. I remember one Friday evening when Jack came by to pick me up to go see a game. I had just gotten home and was preparing to go out again. Jack walked in to find Cassie crying, upset that I was never home, and when I did get home, it was after midnight. True to his role in my family, Jack smoothed things over, consoling Cassie. By the time I came downstairs, she and the situation were calmed.

It was almost impossible not to feel that way in Jack McKinney's presence. You met him for the first time, and you immediately felt that this was a stable guy capable of handling any situation. His reputation was impeccable in Philadelphia coaching circles, and perhaps most prestigiously of all, he had the implicit trust of Jack Ramsay, whom he coached under at St. Joe's and who would later win an NBA championship while assisting Ramsay with the Portland Trailblazers.

Jack was a very solid guy—quirky but solid. We became friends while at St. Joe's, ourselves and our families spending practically every day together.

St. Joe's created my chance to become a full-time basketball coach. After two years of coaching the freshman team and being McKinney's assistant varsity coach, I was ready for my own job. Our archrival, La Salle College, was looking for a new coach after the great Tom Gola had resigned to become city controller of Philadelphia.

La Salle had a talented team but had violated NCAA recruiting rules in the past. The school had been put on probation and was looking for a knight in shining armor to clean things up. Almost incredibly, my lack of experience proved to be my greatest asset. At thirty years of age, I was clean, with no record of having done anything bad, no blemishes whatsoever, well, save for the fact that I was from their archrival, St. Joe's. They could mold me to do things the right way. I needed La Salle, and La Salle needed me.

Not only had Jack McKinney given me my first college job at St. Joe's, which made my first college head coaching position possible, but he had also gotten me my first job coaching in San Juan, Puerto Rico, in the summer. This would have a huge effect on the development of my fast break system.

Back then, in the early seventies, Puerto Rico was a hotbed for coaches from the mainland to head over and experiment. So many well-known coaches took part, everyone from Rollie Massimino to Phil Jackson, Jack McKinney, Del Harris, Jim Lynam, and me.

The situation in Puerto Rico for basketball was wide open. Players were allowed to compete in the summer, because the Superior League was sanctioned as an Olympic development program. Consequently, players from the United States who had any Puerto Rican bloodline could play thirty-five games and remain NCAA eligible. Many of the teams had paid professional players who did not go to college and were the core of the franchise. As a result, the Puerto Rican league was a professional operation, similar to the NBA. Coaches from the states were hired to win games and bring championships home to the local fans in San Juan, Ponce, or Bayamon.

It was also very competitive, and failure to win was quickly dealt with. The coach was sent home; hopefully, with a paid airline ticket. On a few occasions, I received a visit from the owner saying, "Coach, the boys . . ."

This was his way of saying, "You didn't win enough games, and the players are tired of you. Go home."

The way it worked was you took a job coaching a Puerto Rican team. While you were there, you inevitably had some offense or defense or play or press that you had been thinking about all year but didn't want to try out during the regular season, so you would try it out there in the summer. It was a place to experiment with things in basketball that you'd never done.

I wanted to experiment with the fast break—that is, running the fast break all the time. When I got there, however, I found they were already doing that. I mean, I can't say who led whom. They were playing the speed game that I had never seen before.

At La Salle, I had been teaching the usual—bring the ball down under control, pass it five times, and then take a balanced shot. One of the guiding principles of the old Bobby Knight motion offense is that after the fifth pass, the defense begins to break down. Puerto Ricans said, "On the first pass, shoot!" So if I was experimenting in Puerto Rico, it wasn't *on* the Puerto Ricans but *with* them.

My coaching experience in Puerto Rico helped me become a committed fast break believer. The players enjoyed the speed game; get the ball and shoot it quick was their mantra. Early on, I realized that playing fast improved their shooting ability. Defense was ignored in favor of the quick shot.

In Puerto Rico, I learned that a player's shooting ability rises with speed of play. In the United States, players are taught to shoot under control. Don't rush and shoot off balance. Take your time and allow your teammates to get you an open shot with their precision play action.

Puerto Rican players wanted the ball early in the offensive possession to shoot quickly ahead of the defense. In Puerto Rico, controlled, patterned offense was a sign of missed opportunity. Shooting the ball in five seconds was their goal, not running a play and shooting in thirty seconds. After coaching in Puerto Rico for several summers, my motto became "Shoot in five seconds or less."

In addition to learning speed basketball in Puerto Rico, I experienced wild and sometimes violent crowds. After coaching in Puerto Rico, nothing in a sellout arena at home could ever distract me. I had seen it all. In the summer of 1972 my team was in the playoffs against the Bayamon Cowboys. We had a one-game lead and now were to play on Bayamon's home court. Many of the teams played outdoors in the baseball stadiums; however, Bayamon played indoors. The gym held about three thousand fans, who arrived early to snag a coveted seat.

As we entered the arena, the house was already full, with thousands outside jeering at us. The locker room was under the court, and the only path to the floor was a trapdoor. Once on the court, the team was enclosed, floor to ceiling, with a chicken wire fence. The fans were flush next to the fence but unable to throw large objects onto the court. They did, however, use thin sticks to jab through the chicken wire when the team sat on the visitor's bench.

Just prior to the opening tip, the arena door broke open, and thousands more fans rushed inside. And just like that, the arena held *six* thousand.

Five minutes before the game, the fans started chanting, "Teto, Teto, Teto," for their star player, Teto Fluentes. Teto always arrived late to put the fans in a frenzy. Coming up through the trapdoor, he was like the matador entering the ring. It was now game time; however, the referees had not arrived. One half hour later the officials climbed through the trapdoor.

One of the American referees came over to me and said, "Paul, I don't want any shit from you tonight. Sit down and be quiet. As I left my car, I was shot at twice before entering the arena. The shooter yelled, 'If Bayamon loses, we won't miss on the way out.'" I could tell by the look on his face, we were in for a long night. My team ran our fast break offense to perfection. We were leading most of the game, but Bayamon pulled ahead and won by 4 points. My team played well. The speed game was clicking on all cylinders. But we were not Superman; we were not faster than a speeding bullet.

During this same time, I was introduced not only to Puerto Rican–style basketball but also to a coach named Sonny Allen, who had won a Division II championship at Old Dominion while utilizing the fast break. I'd asked him about it, and he told me, "Well, it's really simple. If you sit down, I can explain it to you in an hour. This is not a complex deal. But to do it, you have to be a little crazy."

I told him, "Sonny, I'm a little crazy."

The fast break begins with possession of the ball and then an instant outlet pass to the point guard, who races the ball down court. As the ball speeds down to the offensive end, all five players are sprinting all out to spots on the floor around the basket. This last point cannot be overstated— the players must *sprint*.

The key to the fast break system is to run as fast as possible on every offensive possession. You can't run once in a while and expect the speed game to work. You must repeat the fast pace over and over until the defense begins to break down. The opponent will keep up with you for the first half, but in the second half, they will begin to tire and break down. It's no fun sprinting back on defense one hundred times a game. Eventually, you give up, and then the fast break offense crushes you. The challenge is to repeat the speed game every offensive possession. Slowing down to catch your breath allows the opposition to do the same. It's got to be speed over and over, and when you feel tired, go faster.

As the No. 1 player, the point guard speed dribbles the ball to the offensive end; on every possession, he is instructed to pass for a score. The other four players sprint to assigned spots and wait for the ball. When an offensive player receives a pass from the point, he is to shoot the ball. The message on the pass is, "You are open; shoot!"

The fast break system is repeated over and over, every possession, for the entire game, because it only works when you have total commitment from the players. This commitment is almost impossible to obtain, because it is so demanding on every player, both physically and mentally. You must give maximum effort all the time.

For the most part, players will give you total effort on occasion. They will pick and choose when to go all out. Unfortunately, this will not work with the fast break system. Exerting 50 percent of maximum effort in a game running the break will produce less than 50 percent productivity. Even 75 percent effort will produce only about 60 percent success, but delivering 90 to 100 percent effort in games will produce 100 percent success. Your team—no matter what their talents, no matter what the ability of the opponents—will win all their games. A team that has the fast break running through their blood will not fail. They may lose a game on occasion, but the system will bring them right back to winning.

How can I be so certain? Because I have seen it work at every level, with every type of player, both here and abroad.

Well into my coaching career in 2001, I brought my fast break system to Japan. I coached the Panasonic Kangaroos in Osaka. I had all Japanese players plus two American imports: Mark Sanford and David Booth, both exceptional college players who had a cup of coffee in the NBA.

Despite the language barrier, my team quickly caught on to my scheme. Another advantage of simplicity, it's easy to teach. My Japanese players immediately took to the system and ran, full bore, to their assigned spots. Finally, a team to run my system, and they wouldn't slow down!

Not surprisingly, my challenge was to get my two Americans to follow suit. They were my best basketball players by far—best shooters, best defenders, best all-around skills—but both Sanford and Booth wanted to play at what they thought was a normal pace, sometimes playing fast, sometimes walking it up on offense.

Teaching the Japanese players the speed game was easy; they wanted to please. Teaching my American players was hard; they wanted to enjoy life and make money. Because of the language barrier, the Japanese players smiled and did their work. After every practice, the players would assemble in front of me and bow.

The American players were much more social. We would talk every day about life in Japan. Cassie went on day trips with David Booth's family. But the fast break system missed perfection because of the two American players who wanted to play "normal." As a result, we were an average team. If our Americans scored, we won. Our fast break was not consistent enough to blow teams away.

Midway through the season, we had the All-Japan Basketball Championship, featuring more than one hundred teams from all over Japan. During these games, only Japanese players were allowed to play. Because only my Japanese players were playing, the difference in our fast break was nothing short of stunning. We ran the speed game to perfection. My Japanese players ran the offense over and over. We were unstoppable.

From a mediocre team, the Panasonic Kangaroos became the best in all Japan.

We advanced to the final game, winning all our games by more than 20 points. Ironically, without our two best players, the Americans, we won every game, executing the fast break system. We lost the championship game to the Aishin Sea Horses, who had two American players who were naturalized Japanese citizens. Their added strength and experience were too much for my all-Japanese team. Nonetheless, our players knew that by running the speed game, they could challenge anyone. The fast break raised their level of play.

THE SECRET OF the system, if it really is a secret, is simplicity. You can learn it in a couple of practices. It is not a complex set of offensive plays that change with the defense. The speed game involves running to your spot ahead of the defense and shooting the ball. That's it. The key, and usual stumbling block, is that it must be done all out and every time, over and over, for one hundred times a game. Henry David Thoreau said the key to life is simplicity. "Our life is frittered away by detail," he wrote in *Walden.* "Simplicity, simplicity, simplicity! I say, let your affairs be as two or three, and not a hundred or a thousand." Henry David would have made for a hell of a shooting guard in my system.

The enemy of my system is thinking and strategy and adjustments. Run to your spot as fast as you can; do it over and over from the beginning to the end of the game. No changing positions, no variation, no adjustments to different defenses, no change whether up 20 points or down 20 points. Run the fast break the same over and over; simplicity, simplicity, simplicity.

This system allows the players to perform free and easy. There is no decision when they receive a pass. They are not expected to check the defense or look for an open teammate or wait for a play call from the coach; no, no, and no. There is only one option: shoot.

Once a player has only one option, there's a feeling of being relaxed and ready to release the shot. It happens so quickly that there is no time for second guessing. The point guard passed you the ball with a message: "Fire away!" As the ball is released toward the basket, the other four players are crashing to the rim, collecting a possible missed shot. They are coming from different spots on the court, allowing someone to rebound a miss. The No. 2 always sprints the right side of the court; No. 3 sprints the left side; No. 4 sprints down the middle to the basket; and No. 5 sprints the middle, trailing No. 4's path as the point guard speed dribbles, looking for an open teammate.

All of this takes a few seconds to have five players ready to shoot and also rush to the basket for a possible missed shot. The system works because someone is going to get an open shot ahead of his defender and, more importantly, someone is going to get an offensive rebound for an easy put-back score. The speed game gets you open shots, but more importantly, it gets your team open rebounds for an easy score. We don't care if we make the first shot as long as it provides an easier second shot. The key to success in my fast break system is offensive rebounding, not necessarily proficiency in outside, three-point shooting.

But returning to my conversation with Sonny Allen, he told me that anyone could put in a fast break offense; the problem was that no one wanted to sustain it. He understood that running this fast break offense a couple of times was okay but that it was the repetition. It's the eighty-second and eighty-third time when the other team finally says, "No mas, I've had enough!" But if you don't get to eighty-three, you get your ass kicked, and if that happened enough, Sonny explained, you'd soon discover the fast break offense's worst aspect: "It'll get you fired."

Of course, in the beginning, everyone says they want to run the break, but soon they, coaches and players alike, usually give up. For players it's simple: the fast break takes a physical and mental toll. You not only have to perform all the aspects of the break every time, but you also have to do them running as fast as you can each time. *As fast as you can.* Most players can't do that and *won't* do that.

For coaches, deep down they believe that they are supposed to be constructing plays, that they need to give order to the chaos that basketball can become. No one wants to hear that their team looks disorganized or looks like its playing street ball. No coach ever wants to be accused of "just rolling the balls out."

Coaches believe that they are hired to be chess players, two coaches countering each other with set offenses and defenses, with the players being the incidental actors of the strategy.

But I had begun to question this, to ask that existential question of my coaching life: What am I?

During a La Salle College practice, we threw the ball in to my starting point guard, Charlie Wise, against a full-court press defense. Like all coaches, I had this scheme: reverse the ball, bust somebody up the middle, spread the offense, and throw three or four clever passes, beat the press. Well, something happened, and the play broke down. So I went to talk to Charlie, and he said, "Coach, just let me catch the ball, and I'll just go." From that moment, we never made another pass. We threw the ball to our point guard and let him take care of it.

I was coming to believe that coaches were all too quick to fall in love with schemes and strategies while forgetting that players actually play and win games. Increasingly, my style depended on players, not schemes.

5

Enjoy the Ride

When I came to La Salle College in 1970, it was a school that had just spent two years on NCAA probation for recruiting violations that included paying players. The major reason for me getting the job was to lead them out of the mire of corruption to respectability. I was an assistant coach at St. Joseph's College, coming off a 20-2 record with the freshmen team.

The St. Joe's Hawks were LaSalle's archrival, but no one questioned the quality and respectability of its program led by Jack McKinney and, before him, Jack Ramsay. So out of their dire need to have a knight in shining armor, La Salle went to their bitter enemy and hired me. The mandate from the athletic committee was, at all cost, to get our program back on the straight path.

Gradually, with patience and straightforwardness and a very good first year with a bid to the National Invitation Tournament, we began to get local Philadelphia high school players. The doors were open for the high school recruit to examine the merits of La Salle and to have his parents willing to trust our program with their son. In this area of respectability, I don't think anyone at La Salle College ever questioned my achievement, but after it had been established, they began to want much more.

The alumni wanted another NCAA championship like they had with Tom Gola back in the mid-1950s. Some of them didn't give a hoot about NCAA regulations; they were only concerned with winning. This situation is not unique with La Salle; the cycle runs true to form on many campuses. The university will tolerate high-grade respectability with midgrade wins and losses for only so long, and then it will demand the reverse.

For a few years, it will enjoy maximum winning success and overlook respectability, until there is a smear against the university. Then the cycle continues with a return to honor first and winning a little later on in the program. It is very important for incoming college coaches to know at what part of the cycle they are climbing aboard.

Fortunately, I didn't have to recruit perhaps the finest player I would ever have at La Salle, or at any level for that matter.

Ken Durrett, a six-foot-seven forward from Pittsburgh, was waiting for me upon my arrival. You may have never heard of him, but in his day, he was one of the top two or three college players in America, at a time when the likes of Lew Alcindor, Elvin Hayes, and Bill Walton were playing.

How good was Ken? Since 1955 perhaps the most valued award in Philadelphia basketball is the Robert V. Geasey Trophy, given to the most outstanding player in Philadelphia's Big 5 schools—La Salle, Penn, St. Joseph's, Temple, and Villanova. Winners of the award include a who's who of great college players and pros, including the likes of Hall of Famer Guy Rodgers and local legends like Ed Pinckney and Jameer Nelson. But in all that time, only four players have won the award three times. Ken was one of those players. I have no doubt in my mind that Ken would have gone on to NBA superstardom if not for a knee injury suffered his senior year. To give you an idea of how good Ken was, he was still selected fourth in the NBA draft, even with a catastrophic knee injury, just on the hopes that he could return to his old form.

With Ken as my star player, I went to scout Western Kentucky, who was ranked fourth in the country at the time. I was overwhelmed by their talent, featuring All-American Jim McDaniels, and told my team we were going to slow down and try to control their explosive style of play, though, in my heart, I knew we had no shot.

In practice, my players followed my cue to slow down and take the air out of the ball. In the locker room at the Philadelphia Palestra, Ken Durrett asked if we could press on defense after made baskets. I said okay, figuring we weren't going to score much against this dominant team.

Do anything to make your players feel good before the slaughter.

When the game began, we got the opening tip, and Ken Durrett scored a driving lay-up. We then full-court pressed as planned and stole the ball and scored again. Three minutes into the game, we were ahead 18–2. I stood up to get my team under control, and my assistant, Paul Gallagher, pulled me aside and said, "Sit on the bench and enjoy the ride."

We defeated Western Kentucky 91–76 with a classic run-and-gun basketball that I had nothing to do with coaching. "Coach" Ken Durrett showed me what the speed game can do. It was a lesson learned and used over and over in my coaching career. Let players like Bo Kimble, Diana Taurasi, and Ken Durrett play free and easy, and they will show you the way to victory. Ken scored 45 points that night against Western Kentucky. It was an individual record for many years at the Palestra. In his own way, Ken Durrett was a key architect in my fast break system.

My players at La Salle were mostly Philadelphia-area kids who were a cut below the local star who went to North Carolina or local powerhouses such as the University of Pennsylvania and Villanova, but they equal to anyone in desire and effort. It was fun coaching six-foot-four centers such as Jim Crawford and watching him rise for the occasion and block Howard Porter's jump shot, who was Villanova's six-foot-nine superstar. It was fun grooming your own big man who wasn't good enough to be recruited by the biggies and seeing him develop over four years to eventually win a game against a team that laughed at him in high school.

Don Wilber was a near-seven-footer who was turned down by the major basketball programs as not being ready for the big time and who came to us to help him get there. Even landing an obscure big man was difficult; you needed a little luck. In his senior year, I went to see Don against the best high school team in the area—Abington High. The game was a sellout, and many college coaches from all over the country were there. If Don had a decent game, we would never get him. What a way to recruit, going to see a prospect and hoping he plays poorly so you can get him.

Fortunately for us, this is what happened to Don Wilber. He was introduced as the starting center, and all the college scouts eagerly watched him gracefully as a bird float to center court. Unfortunately for Don, he got his foot caught in his warm-ups and fell on his face in front of three thousand jeering Abington fans. Some of the college coaches who came to watch Don Wilber left then, certain he could never play for their program. Don was mortified. I was elated, because I just discovered my next star.

It took three years to develop Don into a player, but I wouldn't have traded that experience for anything. This awkward giant, nicknamed Big Bird, became a legitimate big-time center who personally beat some of the very coaches who laughed at him in high school and who made a quick exit after his flop a few years before.

Don Wilber was the epitome of all that is good about college coaching. I watched him work day after day conquering clumsiness while developing a devastating hook shot. Through hard work, I saw a basketball version of *My Fair Lady*; it was coaching at its best to be Professor Henry Higgins and see a star grow from nothing.

But the greatest thrill was to be a part of seeing a boy become a man. Don Wilber made most of the problems in college coaching palatable. The problems of college coaching are centered on the task of recruiting.

To me, the practice of recruiting is the cause of continual woe for the college coach who must spend most of his waking hours dealing with it. He is a traveling salesman first and a coach second. He must never leave home without his black telephone book of recruits. He can get through the day without his playbook but not without recruiting data.

I recently went on vacation to Hawaii with a college coach who became immediately distraught upon our arrival to this enchanted island because he had forgotten his mailing list of recruits who were programmed to receive postcards from Hawaii. There is never a day of the year when the college coach can free himself of recruiting. My biggest disappointment in recruiting was that after a full year of effort, you would lose a prospect for the most bizarre reason.

My Philadelphia background, with Jack Ramsay as my mentor, had me coach my team to be smart, controlled, and conservative. I followed the proven ways of winning, especially hard-nosed defense, believing that it would make my team successful. But I had something inside me that rebelled against the "correct" way of playing the game.

I had seen moments of speed and wanted more. I had seen defense that took risks and wanted more. During the 1973–74 season, my La Salle team was playing Temple University at the Palestra arena in a Big 5 game. Temple's coach, Don Casey, was a good friend of mine, and we both wanted bragging rights for the year. Temple went up 10 points, and with five minutes remaining in the first half, they went into a stall and refused to attempt a shot. With no shot clock at that time, Temple could run out the time without taking a shot. To retaliate against Casey's stall, I sent a player named Mo Connelly down to the other end of the court. Mo stood under our basket, and my other four players defended Temple's team. Under Casey's instruction, Temple still held the ball, not attempting to score even with a man advantage.

I countered by sending another player down the court to be with Mo Connelly. Now it was five against three, and the fans were going crazy. No team had ever done this, and Temple was still not trying to score. Finally, with a nod from Coach Casey, their point guard drove to the basket and attempted to score. The stall was over. We were once again playing fast. The fans loved it. At halftime we were still losing, but everyone was cheering for my team, and Don Casey's Temple team was jeered as the villains. Temple went on to win the game, but I made my mark as a coach who is crazy enough to experiment and push the envelope.

After further experimentation with only four players on defense, I came up with my version of the box and none. Many teams play some version of four defenders in a zone defense and one player in man-to-man coverage, commonly known in basketball as a box and one. I decided to follow the four defenders in a zone with the fifth player able to roam full court trying to steal the ball from the guard advancing the play. The idea was to run at the ball handler and give your best attempt at a steal. If unsuccessful, keep going the other way toward your basket.

In 1978 La Salle was playing Duke University at the Spectrum in Philadelphia, with a sellout crowd of eighteen thousand fans. It was a special game featuring two top Philadelphia high school stars: La Salle's Michael

Brooks from West Catholic High and Duke's Gene Banks from West Philadelphia High.

A few years before, I had recruited Banks. I had called his coach, an old friend, and he'd arranged for me to come the following week at 10:00 a.m. to speak with Gene. I showed up, and the coach told me that Gene wasn't going to meet with me. I understood what was going on; that kind of thing happens. But the alumni at La Salle looked at something like this and started to think we were not getting the recruits we should have been getting. But the fact was that we didn't have the clout to attract the likes of Gene Banks, and that made people angry.

Incidentally, about eight years later, when I was coach of the Lakers and preparing for the draft, I called Gene Banks at home to arrange a workout. He wasn't there, and I spoke to his mother, who told me Gene would once again not be able to meet with me, because, this time, he had a wedding to attend. I said fine and hung up. About ten minutes later, my phone rang, and Gene Banks was on the other end, saying, "Coach, when do you need me, morning, noon, night? Just let me know; I'll be there."

The world had changed. I told him what I wanted; of course, what I really wanted to say was "Where was all this enthusiasm when you were at West Philadelphia High?"

The Brooks-Banks game was billed as a heavyweight boxing match. Duke was winning by 15 points with ten minutes to go, when we went to our box-and-none defense and cut the lead to 6. My "none" player was Kurt Kanaskie, who was a terrific outside shooter but a below-average defender.

We had recruited Kanaskie, who came from a very proper churchgoing family outside Harrisburg. Kurt was not a kid who hung out on the corner. North Philadelphia must have been a culture shock to this rural kid. There was nothing in him to make you think he was going to be a very good basketball player. Early in Kurt's first year, he was just another player on a rebuilding team, the last man on a twelve-man squad. Because of his spot, we would grab Kurt and another scrub to play two-on-two with myself and my assistant, Lefty Ervin.

On one occasion, after practice I called Kurt over to play, only this time, Lefty's good friend Billy Magarity was watching practice and asked if he could play in our little half-court game. I said okay, partially because Billy was Lefty's friend but also because Billy's father had given me a new car to drive for the year. The Magarity family had an Audi dealership and were big La Salle alumni. Our little game of two-on-two was going along fine, until out of nowhere Billy Magarity threw a wild elbow at Kurt and knocked him down.

Kurt got up and said to me, "It's okay; don't worry about the hit." I was uncomfortable because Kurt was one of my guys, whom I should defend against the outside world, yet Billy was a friend of the La Salle family. During my hesitation, Kurt looked me in the eye and repeated, "Don't worry; it's going to be okay."

So we resumed the game with Kurt dribbling the ball, being defended by Billy Magarity. Kurt took two dribbles, stopped, dropped the ball, and proceeded to slug Billy in the mouth.

Kurt made his point; he was a man and wasn't going to be bullied by anyone. Billy Magarity, to his credit, took it, realizing he had it coming. The next day in practice, I announced to the team that we were making a change in the starting lineup. Our last player, Kurt Kanaskie, was the new starter because he was tougher than anybody on the team. He started that next game, did well, and started every game for the rest of his career. Kurt turned out to be one of the best shooting guards I have coached in my fast break system. He loved to shoot; he was not afraid of missing. And as I found out in our two-on-two game, he was nasty.

I made him my wild card defender because of that and because, quite frankly, he had little value on defense anyway. After a steal by Kanaskie and a score, we were in the thick of the contest.

Kanaskie attempted another steal in the backcourt and missed, and instead of going down to his basket, he came back to half court and pleaded, "Coach, let me come back and play defense. We have a chance to win this game." I stood up, pointed to our basket, and said, "I command you to go down court. You never wanted to play defense anyway. Don't start now."

Like a good soldier, Nasty Kanaskie followed orders and stayed down on offense. Even though Kurt Kanaskie loved a good fight, for this game all he had to do was shoot.

Unsurprisingly, Kurt went on to have a long, successful career as a coach himself, which included a Division I head coaching position at Drake as well as assistant positions at South Carolina; Penn State; and fittingly for a guy as tough as him, at both Navy and Air Force.

As my existential crisis continued, I began experimenting with techniques outside basketball. For instance, I tried to apply cybernetics to the art of shooting the ball. I lectured my players to mentally picture the ball going in the basket. On the practice court, I had our players shoot free throws with their eyes closed. On several occasions, before the start of the season, we practiced eyes-closed free throws, and I found that many players were actually better shooting with their eyes closed. The drill was fun and had no penalty if you missed; therefore, players were so relaxed that they let it fly with surprising success. Still, once the season started, I abandoned my cybernetic drill for a more practical one of shooting ten normal free throws to end practice.

Late in the season, we were playing Villanova at the Palestra since all key games were played on the University of Pennsylvania campus. The game was sold out, and it came down to the last possession. We had the ball with twelve seconds in the game and were down 1 point. I called for our star player, Michael Brooks, to shoot just before the buzzer. With three seconds left, he missed; there was a mad scramble for the ball, which ended up being a jump ball at our foul line.

With one second remaining, the Villanova player tipped the ball toward half court. Two players dove for the loose ball and collided just before the buzzer signaling the end of the game. The official looked down at the two players and called a foul on the Villanova player, Joe Rodgers, in favor of my player Darryl Gladden. This resulted in a one-and-one free-throw situation for my team. This meant my freshman player Gladden would go to the line, down 1 point with no time remaining, and shoot one free throw, and if he made it, he'd shoot another. If he missed the first shot, the game would be over and Villanova would win.

Before the free-throw attempts, Villanova's coach, Rollie Massimino, called a time-out to ice my young shooter. As Darrell went to the free-throw line, Rollie called a second time-out to double ice him. Rollie looked down at me as if to say, "What advice are you going to give the kid now?"

Rollie and I had had a competitive relationship over the years. He was the fiery, flamboyant coach who would win an NCAA national championship, and I was the quiet nutty professor who was always messing with the game. In this circumstance, it looked like he had me. During the second time-out I was speechless. The team huddle was silent. Finally, Darryl Gladden said aloud, "Coach, do you want me to shoot the free throw with or without?" I was clueless. "Darryl," I said, "what are you talking about?" He said, "Do you want me to shoot it with my eyes open or closed?" I smiled and shot back at him, "Roll your own."

As he went to the line for the third time, I turned to my assistant Lefty Erwin and said, "This game is over; he's going to make both free throws." Darryl went to the line and cradled the ball, and then he looked over at me and grinned.

He proceeded to make the first one to tie the game and the second to win it. Chaos immediately broke out in the Palestra as we beat Villanova by 1 point. I never did find out whether Darrell shot the free throws with his eyes open or closed.

6

Go West, Young Man

During the summer of 1979 my major concern was having a great season at LaSalle. This was the last year of my second four-year contract, and there were signs that the college had grown tired of me. If we didn't have a twenty-win, tournament-bound team, I wouldn't have to worry about moving up the coaching ladder; I was going to be moved out.

The threat of being fired hurt me deeply. I couldn't understand why a college to which I had given eight years of a good, sound, respectable basketball program would throw it away to quell the murmuring of some unhappy alumni who yearned for a return to the days of Tom Gola and NCAA championships. Gola, one of the greatest college basketball players ever, had led the Explorers to the championship in '54 and a return to the NCAA finals in '55. But many of the alumni didn't give a hoot about NCAA regulations; they were only concerned with winning.

This was the cycle I found myself in going into my ninth season at LaSalle. The pressure was on to win big, and the priority of respectability was put in limbo. I had returned the school some of its lost basketball honor, and now they wanted gold crowns or my hide. This situation is not unique to La Salle; the cycle runs true to form on many campuses.

I believed my coaching had brought La Salle as far up the scale of success as they could possibly expect, yet they wanted more. I couldn't stomach the thought of being fired by a college that should have been proud of my work. The situation had led to my own strange, borderline-paranoid feeling that the school and its supporters were actually waiting—rooting—for the team to falter, as final evidence to fire me.

I was ready for the challenge. This was going to be a great year. After a successful season, the recruits would follow, and so would a new four-year contract. In preparation for a successful recruiting year, I was working the summer-camp scene. The best spot for quality high school senior players was the Five-Star camps, where the bluest of blue-chip recruits could be seen. It was while attending one of these talent shows in Pittsburgh that I received a call from Jack McKinney, who was running a boys basketball camp in nearby Milan . . . Italy. He wanted me to fly over the next day and take his place, because the Lakers had called him to Los Angeles for a coaching interview. I was so happy to get away from sitting like a mannequin in the bleachers; I jumped at the opportunity to travel around the world to fill in for Jack.

There were several reasons why Jack would call me. First, I had directed this same camp the summer before, and so I knew the whole routine. Second, Jack had been providing me with job opportunities for several years; he was the one who got me started in college coaching by hiring me as his assistant coach at St. Joseph's College. During my first year at St. Joseph's, Jack had an opportunity to coach in San Juan, Puerto Rico, but couldn't go because of his duties as athletic director. He handed the job to me, and once again, I was working a new basketball job because of Jack McKinney. The next summer, Jack was offered a different coaching position in Ponce, Puerto Rico. He said it was not possible unless they split the job and hire me for half the season, and once again, Jack McKinney had gotten me a job.

In fact, it was Jack who set up my interview with Loyola of Los Angeles in 1979 and met me at LAX, his arm and leg bleeding from a fall while getting the rental car. In trying to help me get a coaching job, Jack had fallen and hurt himself.

I met Jack in the Milan airport as he was departing for Los Angeles and wished him good luck. I knew Jack was happy with his life as an assistant coach with the Portland Trailblazers, but the Lakers job with Kareem Abdul-Jabbar was too attractive to turn down.

After a week of instructing basketball through an Italian interpreter—"*Bloccare!*" ("Block out!")—Cassie and I spent a week vacationing in Paris. We saw nothing in the international papers linking Jack to the Lakers and feared he had lost out. The day I returned from Europe, Jack called and said he was just offered the Lakers job and that an announcement would be made tomorrow. He then asked me if I would I come out and be his assistant. Even though I was looking forward to my showdown season at LaSalle, I instantly saw the chance for a fresh start. It took me about thirty seconds to say yes.

As Jack was working out the details of my position with the Lakers, I called LaSalle's president, Brother Patrick Ellis, to inform him of my decision to leave. He was very gracious and understanding. He told me it was a great opportunity and that the college would gladly release me. I had the feeling he was happy to be rid of me; the alumni now would be off his back. There would be no need to either reward me with a new and bigger contract if we won or fire me if we lost. There was a strong tone of relief in his voice as he wished me good luck in my trek across the country. During my first year with the Lakers, I often thought of that farewell conversation. Their happiness with my timely departure gave me a great deal of hurt. Whenever the Lakers returned to Philadelphia, I always felt uneasy and couldn't wait to repay my Philadelphia connections with a big Lakers triumph.

Jack McKinney asked me to come to LA as soon as possible. The pro summer league was in its last week, and it was a good opportunity to see the rookies, especially our first-round pick, Magic Johnson. I arrived in LA and went immediately from the airport to rookie practice at Inglewood High. This was the first step of my new coaching career, and I was anxiously awaiting my initiation with professional players. From the distance of a college campus, I had an image of them as know-it-alls who were only concerned with bank accounts and who had no interest in being taught anything about the game. I expected them to be uncooperative, undisciplined, and unenthusiastic for the game and their coaches. Everyone knew the pros didn't play hard until the last few minutes of the game, so it was obvious they didn't practice hard. With this picture in mind, I walked on the court with Jack to meet the rookies.

I was immediately greeted by Magic Johnson, who came running over and threw his arms around me, his broad smile of approval signaling to teammates that this college coach from back east was to be accepted.

We then went through a two-hour practice with as much effort and enthusiasm as I ever witnessed in college. I was anxious to find out just how much the professional game had to offer that was not apparent to outsiders, including college coaches.

After practice, I went into the locker room to speak further with Magic and find out the reason for his friendly greeting. I hadn't won any NCAA titles or been named coach of the year, so why the open welcome? He informed me we had a mutual friend in Chuck Daly, who was then an assistant coach with the Philadelphia 76ers and who told him I was a good guy and good coach and that Magic should help me fit into the LA scene. Coincidentally, Magic Johnson was not only the first player I spoke to with the Lakers but also the last Laker I spoke to in a small locker room in Salt Lake City before I was fired.

THE MIGRATION FROM Philadelphia to Los Angeles proved to be difficult for my family. My oldest daughter, Monica, had to leave an established position on the Upper Darby High School tennis team to struggle to make the junior varsity at Rolling Hills High, home to Tracy Austin—the then-defending U.S. Open singles champ—and many aspiring Tracys.

In Drexel Hill we had a beautiful suburban home surrounded by giant sycamore trees and a spacious backyard; we sold the property for a whopping $70,000 and looked to find something comparable in Southern California. A real estate broker recommended by Philadelphia Eagles coach Dick Vermeil showed my wife some properties in Venice. Cassie was distraught to find that there were beat-up properties in less desirable locations going for about $200,000. Anything attractive was well over $400,000! We finally settled on a condominium in Palos Verdes because it was in a great school district and the McKinneys had bought a home nearby. It was more than double the price of our large Drexel Hill home, but it was the best we could afford. Well, actually, we couldn't afford it; to swing the deal, we would need a loan from my new boss, Lakers owner Jerry Buss. I asked for some financial help in securing a home in this crazy land of escalated prices. Buss, who had made the millions he used to buy the Lakers through real estate investing, suggested a scheme that proved to be prophetic. He offered to give me my playoff share in advance, since he was convinced we were going to win the NBA championship that year. My contract, which was still unsigned, called for me to receive one half share. If we won the world title, a share would be worth approximately $30,000. So before we played a game, Jerry Buss offered to advance me a full share, which I thought was very generous.

There was, however, an unexpected twist in the financial aid. While we were at training camp in Palm Springs, Jerry Buss's secretary filled me in on the terms of the advance. It was *not* an advance. It was a loan. That was the first I heard about it. I recalled my discussion with Buss and did not remember anything about him *lending* me the money. It was an advance payable to him only if we didn't win it all. His secretary said he had to charge me, but it was a terrific rate of interest of approximately 7 percent. I was still pleased, because no one else would give me the money, but I made a mental note that everything didn't come out exactly the way it was said. Even though I still thought this was a generous gesture by Buss, my brain was warning me that in La-La Land, things were not always what they seemed to be.

Jack McKinney had to plead with Lakers management to get more money to facilitate my family's move. The Lakers front office intimated that was Jack's problem, since he could have hired plenty of assistant coaches who lived much closer. For the first few days, we were living out of a Marriott, renting a car to go to the Forum and rookie practice. When both of our families arrived in September for the start of school, Jack eased the expense demands by renting an apartment and bringing both families under the same roof. With twelve people in a three-bedroom apartment, it's understandable that the kids labeled it the "insane asylum," but I was impressed and touched by the consideration Jack had shown me and my family.

I REMEMBER GETTING started in my new office at the "Fabulous Forum" and discovering that it was little more than a small closet with two desks for three people. I was to share the space, or lack thereof, with our trainer Jack Curran and previous coach Jerry West, who now held the title of special consultant to Jerry Buss.

In college coaching, your office management had to be top rate, because you were trying to impress recruits. At LaSalle College I had an efficient, well-trained network of letter writing and telephone calls akin to a corporate sales department. In college, if your office procedures weren't sharp, you lost recruits and consequently games; a proficient letter-writing system to recruits was a more valuable coaching tool than an ingenious out-of-bounds play.

But to my utter shock, there seemed to be no system whatsoever with the Lakers. The first telephone call I attempted to make revealed that in order to call outside LA, I had to tell the Forum operator whom I was calling and the nature of the call. I considered my day a success if I could convince the switchboard operator that my call was worth placing—of course, that is, if there was an available line, which frequently there was not.

One of my first tasks was to locate a motivational film for training camp. I had used a Houston Oilers film with my La Salle team, and Jack asked me to track it down. I contacted NFL Films, and they told me we could have the film for a $150 rental. Because of the squeeze being put on Jack by Lakers officials, he told me to cancel our order. I pleaded with him to get the film, because Bum Phillips did a great job of showing how teamwork leads to a successful program. The theme was "Don't let go of the rope," and it showed how, as with mountain climbers, everyone on the team is dependent on others for success. Embarrassed, I canceled our order, and I was a bit disturbed that we couldn't swing such a small transaction.

When I took to letter writing as a means of communicating, I found that the only available writing paper didn't match the envelopes. I was told not to worry, that when the remaining stock of a few hundred envelopes was used up, they would reorder some in the same color as the stationery. We finally got the telephone and stationery inadequacies straightened out but never to the Madison Avenue–like style of a college office. I later learned that the simpler style of the Lakers and the rest of the NBA was better than the competitive approach of major college basketball programs.

Our immediate office task was to prepare for training camp and the season. I remember having lengthy discussions with Jack about what offenses and defenses would be best for this team. He was convinced that the set offense must revolve around Kareem but that Kareem must be an effective passer as well as scorer. Jack believed he could design an offense similar to what he had in Portland with Bill Walton, when the Trailblazers won the NBA championship.

The only area in which Jack and I would constantly disagree was the fast break. My attempt to influence the direction of the team was to make them more of a running group. My college background had established me as a relentless fast break coach and the creator of what had become known in Philadelphia as "the system." When it was good, it was forty minutes of nonstop fast break basketball, and when it was not, my critics called it the "septa system," a reference to the less than highly regarded public transit system in Philly.

Jack was somewhat apprehensive of my commitment to the running game; he wanted to run but not with the emphasis and magnitude that I did. He tempered my suggestions as we prepared for the season and politely let me know that too much emphasis on the break was not in his game plan.

I disagreed with him, because I felt that there were great opportunities for success with the fast break in the NBA. I argued that pro teams were slow in getting back to play defense and that a quick, relentless fast break would reap innumerable easy shots and bring winning basketball. Only the Boston Celtics of the Bill Russell era had capitalized on a continuous fast break push, and Russell ended up with more championship rings (eleven) than fingers. Most teams ran the fast break only when it was readily available, like off a steal. My approach was to run the ball down court on all occasions, both after misses and made baskets of the opponent.

Jack believed that veteran players would not accept a relentless running game. I countered that this was the very reason why we should install the running game. I argued that if the offensive team felt it was too demanding to run all the time, how do you think the defensive team—the opponent—would feel about defending it? I felt that a little convincing on our part to have the team run more would pay such dividends in winning games that players would gladly accept the extra work required.

WE WENT TO our first Lakers training camp with an understanding that our running game would be a selective blend of fast pace and slow pace, depending on the circumstances. Jack was anxious to get a feel for the team, especially Kareem, before making any final decisions on the best rhythm for the squad. I was anxious for the start of training camp and the opportunity to work with the best basketball players in the world. I was particularly interested in meeting the NBA's best player: Kareem Abdul-Jabbar. I had heard rumors that he was aloof and difficult to coach. I made the decision not to try to impress him with my basketball knowledge but rather to go nice and slow, waiting for Kareem to ask for help. That was a good decision on my part, because Kareem was a very cautious person who was not easily impressed. He was a sensitive guy who noticed everything going on around him and after careful evaluation would make decisions on whether you were real or phony.

My first coaching encounter with Kareem happened several days into training camp. We were having difficulty getting the ball inside to Kareem in our offense, and both the passer and Kareem were showing signs of frustration. Jack McKinney had me do a mini clinic on the art of passing the ball.

I demonstrated how passing is like dancing. The receiver, in this case Kareem, must actively show a target, and the passer must concentrate to deliver the ball precisely on target. The lazy pass is a constant problem in basketball, leading to costly turnovers. My lecture illustrated that this should never happen with a pass to Kareem since his extended arm presents a target above the reach of any defender. Consequently, with care and precision, the passing lane to Kareem should always be open. Kareem responded well to the passing clinic by being more active in showing the target area, and the passers responded favorably to delivering the goods. I pointed out that good passing was like good shooting—both demanded great skill and accuracy. Since all our players were gifted offensive scorers, there was no reason why they couldn't be terrific passers.

Kareem liked the simplicity and effectiveness of my coaching clinic and, from then on, accepted me as a coach. To be a successful coach in the NBA, you must have the support of the key player on your team, or else he will tear down even the best of plans. On the Lakers, Kareem Abdul-Jabbar was *the man*, and therefore his acceptance of me insured a pleasant journey through the season.

As training camp came to a close, Jack had to make final decisions on some players. The situation was particularly difficult at the guard position. We had Norm Nixon and Magic Johnson, but after that it was a dead heat. We decided to keep veteran Ron Boone, who'd had a terrific training camp, while the fourth spot went to rookie Ollie Mack, who impressed us with his raw talent and unlimited potential. The fifth and final spot went to Brad Holland, another rookie, who was recuperating from knee injury and hadn't looked very good in training camp but was a terrific, hardworking kid.

Jack wanted to keep no more than five guards on the roster, and therefore, only one of them could stay as a small forward and backup guard in case of injury. Jack decided to keep Michael Cooper, a young player who seemed to only delight in dunking but who, Jack believed, could be developed into a consistent defensive player.

Most of Cooper's development as an NBA player came under me first as an assistant coach. I befriended Mike and gave him tips on how to get more playing time. Clearly, the route was to become a steady defensive player. We had talented offensive players ahead of him but none with his catlike quickness. All he had to do was work at defense every time down court, and his stock would rise considerably.

We opened the 1979–80 season in San Diego against the Clippers. All the hard work of training camp gets thrown up for grabs for the first win. Even though you play eighty-two games, it's important to win the first, especially when it's your first game ever as an NBA coach. We didn't play very well. The offense was sluggish, and our half-court play sets misfired. Still, with a few seconds left, we trailed just 102–101 and had possession of the ball. In our huddle during the time-out, we called for the ball to go inside to Kareem. Don Ford inbounded the ball and threw a perfect pass to the outstretched arms of Kareem, who caught it at the foul line, turned, and launched a twenty-foot skyhook that ripped through the net as the buzzer sounded.

Magic ran out and picked up Kareem in a rare moment of pure joy. In the locker room, Kareem admitted this was the first time in the NBA anybody ever picked him up celebrating a win. He cautioned that it was a long season and that one win meant little, but the grin on his face revealed that it meant much more to him and to our team.

But things change quickly in the NBA, both on and off the court, and our good fortune in San Diego was soon to sour. Just twelve games later, everything in the Lakers' world would literally and figuratively come crashing down, altering the fortunes and lives of so many forever.

7

Substitute Teacher

Uneasy lies the head that wears a crown.

—WILLIAM SHAKESPEARE, *King Henry IV*

The good fortune of our opening-game victory had quickly soured by game thirteen. We had just lost badly to Golden State and were taking a well-deserved day off, our first since the start of training camp. I called Jack and told him I had reserved a tennis time at my condominium's tennis court for 10:00. Jack said it would take him a few minutes but that he would be over to destroy me on the court.

I went over to the courts to hold our reservation and waited for Jack. He never came. I went back home a half hour later and called Jack's home, but there was no answer. This was not alarming to me. I figured he received a call from the Lakers to do something and couldn't reach me at the tennis court to cancel. My guess was that he had gone to the hospital to see Mike Cooper, who was being examined after a spill in the Golden State game.

It was a few hours later that we received a frantic call from Jack's wife, Claire, telling us Jack had been found in a local hospital as the victim of a bicycle accident that occurred on a steep hill between our homes. Apparently, he went into his garage to drive to my condo, and realizing that his wife had taken the car shopping, Jack decided to hop on his son's bike and keep his tennis date with me. Somewhere in route, he took an awful spill and lay unconscious.

Paramedics were called by a passing motorist, and Jack was brought without identification to Little Company of Mary Hospital. After making several calls to the police in search of her husband, Claire was informed that a man in tennis gear had been rushed to the emergency ward. She knew before she got to the hospital that it must be Jack. After she identified him, she called us and said the doctors were fearful that he may not regain consciousness due to a severe head injury. When Cassie and I arrived at the hospital, Jack's face was cut and bruised almost beyond recognition.

The doctors cautioned us that he may slip away at any moment during the next forty-eight hours, and the agony and apprehension of those hours was nerve-racking. I was permitted to be in the intensive care ward, because Claire had told the nurse I was Jack's brother, which, in many ways, I was. We were close friends who had worked the basketball circuit together for years and now were here in Hollywood to stake our claim. We were in this strange territory and had only each other to rely on. Outside of my family, there wasn't anyone in the world I had a closer tie to than Jack McKinney, and here he was holding on to life by a thread.

The following morning, with no change in Jack's unconscious state, I had to turn my thoughts to Lakers basketball. That very night, we were to play the Denver Nuggets in the Forum. There was a scheduled practice that morning, and if I didn't show up to run it, then no one would. As I drove to practice collecting my thoughts, I realized that there was no one else in the world who could run this team, at this moment, except me. Without Jack McKinney, I was the only one who knew what was going on. The players were very concerned for Jack and went through the motions of practice like robots. Like me, they were going to show up against Denver, but their minds would be elsewhere.

I arrived for my first NBA game as acting head coach with great trepidation. When I accepted the job as assistant coach, I had aspirations to be a head coach after five years. The season was less than five weeks old, and I was thrust into the lead role. Jack McKinney's injury was a freak twist of fate for a person who had worked so hard and so loyally for others. From his dedicated years as a college coach at St. Joseph's to his five years as an assistant in the NBA, Jack McKinney had paid his dues to the game. Now when it was about to pay him back with a golden opportunity in Los Angeles, something horrible had happened.

About an hour before the game, I met briefly with Jerry Buss, who informed me that under the circumstances, I was in charge for tonight's game. He was trying to extend a fragment of confidence to the state of confusion, but I clearly recognized he had no other choice. Within the few hours of Jack McKinney's injury, nothing could be done about the coaching situation. Neither Bill Sharman nor Jerry West wanted to step in and actively take over, so by default, I was it. As I left Jerry Buss's office, I realized this vote of confidence was a very temporary thing. It would last perhaps as long as tonight if we lost or as long as it would take to hire an experienced NBA coach.

The game was a blur. The players were going through the motions, reacting by instinct but not by the desire to play well. We were losing for the entire game, and it looked as though my first defeat was inevitable. Only a stroke of luck could turn this game around, and given the recent circumstances, this wasn't likely. In the closing seconds of the game, Jamaal Wilkes threw up a desperation twenty-foot shot to beat the buzzer, and miraculously, it went in to tie the game and send it into overtime. We then went on to win the game in the extra period and turn a sure loss into a satisfying victory. I often look back to that game and realize that my NBA career was determined by a single shot by Jamaal Wilkes. If he had missed it, I surely would have been gone as acting head coach the next day.

DURING THE NEXT few days, Jack McKinney regained consciousness, and the fear for his life was considerably reduced. The new concern was whether he would recover from his head injury and, if so, how long that would take. To see him and hear his discordant murmurings, you would think he may never be the same. But he had beaten the first crisis, so there were reasons for hope.

I was about to take the team on my first road trip and felt more confident after a three-game winning streak. Jerry Buss talked to me again and said he'd see me when we got back. I got the impression that I was being given the team for this one excursion and that my position as caretaker would then be reevaluated. I felt like a Hertz rent-a-coach who was being given a test drive and who could easily be turned in for another model.

The trip was to be a bumpy ride. We had to play in Seattle against the world champion Sonics; then in Portland against the red-hot Trailblazers, who were the only team to already beat us at home; and finally in Phoenix against the Suns, who had beaten us at home for the past few years. The results were true to form—we lost all three.

My luck had run out. Any notions that this was an easy league to win in were quickly scuttled. Though we played well in all three games, winning in those cities was like hitting the pick-six at Hollywood Park. You can win a few races, but eventually, inevitably, you're going to go home broke. We returned home with a 3-3 record with me as head coach, and the ax was being sharpened. The one thing holding them back from removing me was that Jack McKinney was still in very serious condition and hiring a new coach from the outside would cause unrest with the public. The smart thing to do would be to wait and see just how long Jack would be sidelined. As long as the team could win enough games under me, the Lakers would hold a pat hand. But one more loss and that plan would surely be reviewed and likely revised.

We had a crucial practice session at home before playing Kansas City in the Forum. For the first time, I could sense that the players were evaluating my coaching over the past six games, and like the 3-3 record, feelings seemed split down the middle.

From the start, players such as Norm Nixon and Spencer Haywood were against me, while Jamaal Wilkes and Mike Cooper were behind me. The decision was not yet clear, but before practice ended, the final voice was heard. We were in the middle of a drill, and I was demonstrating to the team how I wanted them to get around a screen on defense. There was a question among the players about whether it was best to go over the top of the pick or slide underneath. I instructed them to go over the top. Kareem Abdul-Jabbar then spoke up and said, "If that's the way you want us to do it, then that is the way it'll be done."

The team leader had spoken. The decision was made. Kareem had demonstrated his approval of my coaching and was telling the players to comply. Without his vote of confidence, we would have floundered back and forth, with different players working for their own personal advantage. Kareem, as *the man*, allowed me the opportunity to coach and get the cooperation of the players. With Kareem's stamp of approval and some good fortune, we could win. Without his acceptance, failure was around the corner.

The coach of the Kansas City Kings was Cotton Fitzsimmons, a well-accepted and very competent coach in the NBA. When we met at the shootaround the day of our game, Cotton was very standoffish to me. I was new; I was Jack McKinney's stand in, a no-account in the coaching world. At least Cotton said hello, which was more than other coaches did as I went through the league. In the college coaching game, you were liked or disliked by opposing coaches but not ignored. But in the NBA, I had no credibility; I might as well have been invisible. We won the next night against Kansas City with a big second-half surge, and with the win, my role as interim head coach was solidified until Jack McKinney was fit to return.

I had gone seven games now, with just me on the bench, and was getting used to it. I had temporarily asked a reserve, Don Ford, to sit next to me and pick out the opponent's play sets, but this didn't work very well since Don was more interested in playing than scouting. I again met with Jerry Buss, and he suggested I get someone to help me temporarily on the bench. I immediately thought of some coaches I knew from my college days, but they were in the middle of their season. And even if they would come to Los Angeles, it might only be for less than a year. No one in their right mind would accept a job under those circumstances.

I was also getting pressure from Jerry Buss to hire his candidate for the position, Elgin Baylor. Buss thought Elgin would be well received by the fans, and besides, Buss had intended to hire him in a public relations capacity anyway. So when his temporary coaching job would end with Jack McKinney's return, Baylor could move along into the Lakers organization.

My choice for an assistant was Pat Riley, currently the color commentator on Lakers broadcasts with Chick Hearn. I had gotten to know Pat during the early weeks of the season and had found him to be likeable and well informed about the NBA game. I felt the need for someone who had been around the league and who could school me on the players. As a former Laker for a number of years, Pat understood the feelings of players. I also wanted someone who was easy to get along with during the long season, and Pat and I soon became good friends.

The only drawback was Pat's total lack of coaching experience. I did not see that as a problem since that was my strong suit after eighteen years of preparation. I could see where it would be a plus to have someone who wouldn't try to outguess you with an out-of-bounds play or technical decision. I presented my feelings to Jerry Buss, and he objected to hiring Pat Riley. He clearly wanted me to go with Elgin Baylor and was politely telling me to do so. But I persisted with my choice, and Buss finally consented, offering these parting words: "I wouldn't pick Pat Riley. But you're the coach, and it's your decision. So okay."

Riley proved to be a good choice for me. He gave me insights into the players' feelings that were beneficial during my first year. I had made a decision to delegate the scouting of our opponents entirely to my assistant. This was my way of bringing some real sense of belonging to him. In this case, it meant Riley was to scout the opponent and then, on the day of the game, deliver to the team his findings. Most head coaches would take the material off the assistant and deliver it himself. I felt differently. I felt as though it made an assistant coach more than a robot and closer to being a real contributor. Pat started this role with great apprehension. He was concerned the players would not give him a chance and would only see him as an ex-player. After a few weeks, Pat became more relaxed and did a very competent job.

But as time went on in the coming seasons, Pat became overly confident in his position and, at times, gave the impression that he knew more than the man who fought to hire him—you know, *me*. I don't think it was intentional on Pat's part, but nonetheless, he became too big for his job.

I also made my assistant in charge of game films. I had Pat prepare video segments for our players to see their strengths and weaknesses. In this area, Pat was an expert. No one did a better job with films than the Lakers.

Through Pat's setup, we had edited tapes of our first-half performance during the halftime break. The whole team could see exactly what plays were hurting us on defense and what offensive sets were working well for us. I allowed Pat to deliver the video version to the team, and then I would wrap things up before going back out on the court.

During my first year, it was difficult adjusting to all the travel. While I was at LaSalle, a big road trip was a four-hour bus ride to Bucknell University in western Pennsylvania or an hour flight to Providence College in Rhode Island. In the NBA a road trip could last two weeks and cover thousands of miles from coast to coast. I had to adjust my coaching to be ready for a game in Chicago on a Tuesday, in Milwaukee on Wednesday, and in Atlanta on Thursday and then be ready to return home for a game Friday night in the Forum.

During the early weeks, Pat was very good at informing me when the players would need a rest and what city would be best to stay an extra night. Only a veteran player has a feel for the travel, and Pat helped to make it a smooth ride.

There were, however, a few bumpy parts of the road during that first season. My first personnel problem was with Spencer Haywood. He had been traded to the Lakers during training camp and was most anxious to assert his influence on the team. Jack McKinney was impressed with Spencer's potential to provide the necessary rebounding alongside Jamaal Wilkes and Kareem Abdul-Jabbar.

Up to the time of Jack's bicycle injury, Spencer had the starting position at power forward, but there were moments even then that the team objected to him. During a game in Seattle, I turned to one of the players on the bench and rhetorically asked, "How could we be down 18 points?" The player quickly replied, pointing to Haywood, "Get him out of the game, and we'll win it."

For the most part, Spencer had worked well with Jack McKinney. Now with me at the helm, Spencer wasted no time in confronting me with his demands for more playing time. I suspect he felt that the sooner he got to the rookie coach and established his part of the turf, the better for Spencer Haywood. After a big win in Houston, he told me he had a deal with

Jack McKinney to be a starter and play over twenty minutes a game. I told Spencer that I was following no deals between him and Jack. I was following only one principle with respect to the players, and that was to play everyone the exact amount it took to win the game. Using that formula, Spencer would play sometimes five minutes and other nights twenty-five minutes, but there were no set guarantees. I told him that minutes played would depend on how well he performed.

This was not sufficient for Spencer, and he informed me that he was going to see Jerry Buss as soon as we arrived back in Los Angeles. The meeting had already been set up, and for the first time, I realized players would circumvent the coach and go directly to the owner with their complaints.

In college basketball, a player would never go to the school president and ask for more minutes. If confronted, the president would immediately refer the player to his coach and allow the coach to deal with the matter entirely. Jerry Buss, however, enjoyed being involved in such issues and relished the opportunity to resolve some matters belonging to the coach. It was his team, and he wanted to take part in its operation.

The meeting between Spencer Haywood and Jerry Buss took place with no immediate impact. A few days later Buss spoke with me about the Haywood matter but did not make demands to give Spencer more minutes. He was anxious to keep the players content and hoped I could do something to cheer Haywood up. I told Buss I would do my best to ease the problem but that I did not like the idea of players going around the coach to the owner to air their complaints and expect him to intervene. On this occasion, Jerry did not step in, but a dangerous precedent was being set that he would welcome players' complaints. This was a wedge that players would use in the future.

A few weeks later in Salt Lake City, Spencer met again with me, requesting more time. I informed him then that he must fill the role of a power forward if he wanted more playing time. I pointed out to him this meant getting more rebounds, especially on the offensive end when either Kareem or Jamaal were shooting. Spencer had been competing with them for outside shots instead of complementing them with some hard follow-up rebounds. Spencer felt that his jump shot would establish himself as a star, as he was on other teams. Unfortunately, on this team there was no room for another star, only a role player. I kind of felt sorry for Spencer. He had always had the lead part in the show, and now it was gone forever. His only survival would have been to accept the understudy's role and be content. His pride, however, was too strong, and he would not accept a smaller role.

I told Spencer in Salt Lake City that he must either willingly be a substitute to help us win or not play and go elsewhere. I had dealt all my cards to him; take 'em or leave the game. The result was that Spencer would, for a time, accept his role but then sulk and complain. His antics on the bench showing disapproval of being there and his run-ins with other players were like the actions of an alcoholic who resolves to be sober but secretly sneaks a few bourbons during lunch. He would promise to be a willing team member, but his actions were those of an angry, frustrated star.

There were times during the season when Spencer made a solid contribution to our team. At times, he would defy defenders and power up inside with the best of them, but on many other occasions, he would sulk and complain. He frequently would forget to play his man, forget our offensive play, and forget to catch the ball before attempting a score.

On one occasion during halftime of a home game, Spencer ripped off his uniform in the locker room and announced that he had had enough and was through. Jim Chones went over and cautioned him not to do that, implying he would be discharged from the team and lose everything. Spencer calmed down and finally put his uniform back on and returned for the second half.

By then, I had had enough of Spencer Haywood and was determined to not play him. After the game, I met with Bill Sharman, our general manager, and Jerry Buss telling them about Spencer's antics. They asked me to wait and let things cool off for a few days, and then if I still thought it best, they would remove him. The following day, we were to leave on a three-game road trip, and I felt as though it was unthinkable for me to bring Spencer along.

One of the reasons I didn't use him in the first half was that Spencer had missed practice due to a mysterious "illness." He said he was jogging on his day off and that the trees and bushes caused an allergy attack. So now I used his story as a way to get him to comply. I told Spencer he must go to the doctor and get a complete medical clearance before rejoining the team. He said it had miraculously cleared up, but I insisted he get a series of medical tests.

We left Spencer back in LA, and I was able to temporarily show him and the team that I was in charge. The players knew Spencer wasn't sick and therefore knew I was responsible for keeping him away. By and large, they were pleased with this action. During that week, I had several long-distance telephone conversations with Bill Sharman discussing the issue. His opinion and that of Jerry Buss was to keep Haywood. Dr. Buss said the way to handle Spencer Haywood was to start him, build up his statistics, make him an attractive player in the NBA, and then trade him. He was, in their opinion, a difficult problem but too valuable to give away. They saw Haywood as a million-dollar property that under present circumstances would only sell in the marketplace for a few coins.

Sharman pleaded with me to back off my demand to trade Spencer and wait for a better time. He also tried to counsel me in how to deal with the Haywoods of the league. You can't, like college, pick and choose who you want. Bill Sharman informed me that no matter how bad a guy is, you have to put up with him and manage to use his talent. I disagreed and believed that you should get rid of a player who is working counter to his team. Sharman was telling me I must learn to put up with the ego problems in the NBA, and for what Haywood had contributed, I couldn't agree. I would be willing to work around the super ego of a Kareem or a Jamaal or a Magic Johnson, because their value to the team was immense, but Spencer Haywood's value was as a supporting actor and therefore expendable.

The Haywood problem was manageable while we were on the road and he was in Los Angeles. Buss had some long discussions with Spencer Haywood and was convinced Spencer would not get out of line. I objected and said Spencer's reform would last a week before he returned to his old ways. Buss felt differently and added that he told Spencer to keep his bags packed because if there was another incident, he would be gone. Buss also informed me that releasing Spencer Haywood, even for a good reason, would cost him around $750,000 in salary. I countered that was nothing if he remained and soured the whole team, which was worth millions. So we compromised that I would keep Spencer and give him an active part in the team while the front office would use this time to go out and trade him. Spencer Haywood was to go but on Buss's terms, when the dollar was right. As a result of this meeting, Spencer Haywood returned to the team as if nothing happened. I was going to play him more now, rather than less, in order to get rid of him.

During this time of turmoil with Spencer Haywood, I later found out that he had plotted to have me killed. Yeah. He hired two hit men from Detroit to do me in. They apparently trailed me for a few days, tracking my path from my home in Palos Verdes to the Forum in Inglewood. Their plan was to run me off the road in the hills of Palos Verdes, making it look like a car accident.

Fortunately for me, during their test runs, Spencer talked to his mother, who sensed something was wrong with her son. She pleaded, "Whatever you are planning on doing, don't do it." Spencer listened to her and sent the potential killers back to Detroit. Years later, Spencer visited me at Loyola Marymount University and asked for my forgiveness. I accepted his apology, and we parted as friends. I felt a rush of joy to be alive sitting next to Spencer. Otherwise, I would have been dead.

8

He Knows That We Know

Intertwined with the Spencer Haywood saga was the situation with Jim Chones. He came to us in a trade with Cleveland for our current backup center Dave Robisch. What evolved was a scramble for the starting forward position between Chones and Haywood. When one faltered, the other was ready to capitalize on the situation.

During the road trip with Haywood getting his "medical checkup" back in LA, Chones had the power forward position all to himself. We played in Chicago, and he was awful. His defense was make-believe, and his effort on the boards was AWOL. At the start of the second half, I tried to run a play for him on offense to get him going, but he ran the wrong play and turned the ball over. We eventually won the game, but no thanks to Jim Chones.

I couldn't figure out why he was playing so poorly now that he had a clear opportunity without Haywood. He now could play full throttle and show us how good he was, and yet he was playing flat. We wound up the trip in Atlanta against the strong front-court duo of Dan Roundfield and Tree Rollins. Prior to the game, I met with Chones and reviewed with him the role of a power forward for our team, how we needed him to be a tough, aggressive rebounder, especially with Jamaal Wilkes and Kareem Abdul-Jabbar taking many of the shots.

Just as Haywood had, Chones objected and said all he does is work for the team without getting any personal glory. To a keen observer, it was obvious Chones was going through the motions, and taking no chances to look bad, he would turn his back while defending a fast break rather than facing it and trying to stop the attack.

For instance, the Atlanta Hawks stole the ball at half court with three players racing to their basket. Only Jim Chones was back to defend their fast break, but before they came close to the basket, Chones ran away from the play, allowing the Hawks to score an easy hoop. Chones didn't get beat by their fast break, because he was nowhere near the basket. My guess is he figured that if he was not around, I couldn't blame him for bad defense.

On our next offensive play, Chones was fouled in the act of shooting and went to the line for two free throws. He shot the first one and focused totally on the rim, and then before the second shot, he looked over at the bench to see our reaction to his previous defensive performance. Riley turned to me and tersely said, "*He* knows that *we* know."

Jim Chones knew we watched him run away from defending the fast break. From that moment on, Jim Chones knew we were aware of his game plan. I remember kidding Pat Riley about what Sharman and Buss would think of me if I told them it's Chones we should get rid of, not Haywood. I never said anything that season, because I knew getting one player out of the program was more than I could expect.

Chones remained our starting power forward for several weeks, until one night in Milwaukee when he and I had a brief but heated argument during a time-out. We had just blown a big lead, and I was attempting to stem the tide. As our team came to the bench, Chones looked at me and said, "What the hell are you looking at?"

Our next practice was at Georgetown University in Washington DC. In preparation for the Washington Bullets, I decided that my consideration of the players' feelings was over, and I must firmly establish some basic rules. I instructed our trainer, Jack Curran, to stretch our squad first, and then I would meet with them in a closed-door session. I anticipated trouble, perhaps blows, so I wanted the team ready to come out immediately and start running.

At the meeting, I exposed Chones and informed him that he was being removed from the starting lineup. Anyone who allowed a personal frustration to interrupt the team goal of winning the game would not be allowed to play. Chones seemed stunned and not sure what to do. There was silence in the room, and I felt that with one wrong word open rebellion could erupt. Breaking the silence was Kareem, who started by saying, "Coach, you must understand the professional athlete," and he paused.

I felt impending doom, with Kareem, as captain, about to defend the actions of Jim Chones. However, he proceeded to condemn not only the antics of Chones but also those of Spencer Haywood and others. He continued by saying that the pro athlete is basically a spoiled star from college who must learn to control his personal aspirations for the good of the team and that unless he does this, his team will never be successful. Kareem took off on my theme and delivered the message far better than I had attempted.

Chones, perhaps as stunned as me, said nothing. Kareem had sealed the decision. This team was in the pursuit of unselfishness and, consequently, winning. Several months after we won the world championship, Peter Vecsey of the *New York Post* commented that my swift handling of the Jim Chones incident was a vital key to our ultimate success and my graduation day as a legitimate NBA coach.

I often wonder if Peter Vecsey knew how accurate he was in placing such importance on a seemingly everyday matter. Of course, the real key was not me but Kareem, who spoke his peace and clearly defended my position. If it truly was my graduation day, the diploma was presented by Kareem Abdul-Jabbar.

We went out the next night with Spencer Haywood in the starting lineup and played a terrific game, only to lose it at the buzzer on a tip-in by Elvin Hayes. The loss, however, could not diminish the accomplishment of the meeting. We were in pursuit of unselfish team play, and nothing was going to stop us now.

ALTHOUGH IT WAS not intentional, the timing of Chones's benching gave me the opportunity to showcase Spencer Haywood as I had agreed. Spencer played hard and, at times, was decent, but too frequently he could not deliver when needed. He seemed to always lose the handle of the ball as it was passed inside to him. In one of our playoff games against Seattle, Magic Johnson made a pass to Spencer underneath the basket for a sure 2 points, but it bounced off his hands as if they were boards. Magic made one glance over to me, and his look said it all—"What is he doing in this game that means so much to us?" I was trying to keep Spencer alive by giving him some minutes, but I knew that Magic was right.

Magic's rookie season provided a dilemma of great magnitude itself, though one with a simpler solution. He was causing some problems with team unity by trying to control the ball all the time. Magic believed he could make things happen when he handled the ball, and he was getting on the nerves of some of the veterans, especially Norm Nixon.

Even when Magic didn't have the ball leading our fast break, he would come running down hollering for the ball, distracting the players ahead of him trying to complete the break. I took him aside during a practice and explained his teammates' displeasure and how he ought to pick and choose his calls for the ball. Magic was stubborn and wanted things to go his way, but he played so hard and wanted to gain the respect of his teammates so much that he listened to me and demonstrated better control.

He also annoyed players when he would choose a fancy pass that would be intercepted rather than a simple pass for a score. Some players believed Magic was showboating his talent at their expense, and they were grumbling. This problem had a happy ending that season, because after I talked to him about making the simple play when it was there, Magic settled into some truly great team basketball.

No one in the league passed the ball or rebounded missed shots better than Magic Johnson. His official acceptance by the team came four months into the season when he had his head ripped open while rebounding a ball over Micheal Ray Richardson. He had to leave the game for temporary wire stitches and then returned to pass and rebound our team to an exciting victory in Madison Square Garden. It was as if our players saw this as his initiation as a true LA Laker. The next day, I kidded him that he was lucky he already had the nickname "Magic," because "Wirehead" now seemed appropriate. If it stuck, "Wirehead" sure would have hurt his endorsements, but it would have been a tribute to his hard effort for his team. By mid-February of his rookie year, Magic Johnson had emerged as the perfect team player, a model of what Kareem had preached weeks before.

Perhaps our greatest single victory of that season was, however, won without the services of Magic. We were in the charmed Boston Garden and getting beaten soundly into the third period, when the team rallied behind the spectacular defensive play of Michael Cooper filling in for Magic, who was suffering from a pulled groin muscle. Cooper gloved Larry Bird on defense, while Kareem destroyed the aggressive Dave Cowens with skyhooks. We won the game at the buzzer with Norm Nixon's clutch foul shooting.

We were like a group of high school kids who had just won a state tournament. Even though it was only one game in a long eighty-two-game season, the joy was real and felt by all. The long flight back to LA was a big party. We had the entire first-class section to ourselves. All the team rules of no music and no drinking were suspended, and players laughed and joked all the way home. Before we touched down, our team was dancing in the aisles with the flight attendants.

I had never experienced such a natural outpouring of joy as that flight from Boston. One trip like that can make up for all the stranded nights spent in airports waiting for the weather to clear. As we deplaned that evening in Los Angeles, you could sense that there was something special about this team. We were going to be heard from in the playoffs.

9

No Thanks

As the season rolled on and the pieces began to fall in place, there was the daily question of Jack McKinney's status. For the first few weeks, he could barely function, but then gradually he got stronger and was home recuperating. Jack was alert enough to realize that he must return to work and take control of his team, but his speech and memory were way behind.

I found myself hopelessly caught in the middle. I was running the team and clearly saw their needs, and I knew Jack was not ready to return. He would only hurt himself by returning to the team in his condition. One or two off-the-wall remarks by Jack and he would lose the players for good. Jack told me of his desire to come back and talk to the team. From watching games on TV, he wanted to clear up what he saw them doing wrong and also compliment them on their fine play. He wanted to tell them to wait; he wouldn't be out much longer.

I knew from listening to him that he wouldn't be able to get the message across effectively. I encouraged him to hold off coming back for a few more weeks. I never faltered in my goal to preserve the team for Jack McKinney, who was responsible for me being in the NBA. I know the circumstances later on in the season clouded the issue, but I know I never wavered in my loyalty to Jack McKinney.

It was early January when Jack insisted on coming to a practice to see the team. One Sunday morning at a shootaround, Jack came and sat up high in the Forum as the team went through its routine. Afterward, we met in the dressing room to watch a film I had ordered. Coincidentally, it was the very Houston Oilers film that Jack had asked me to cancel before his injury. I waited for Jack to come into the locker room, but he was nowhere in sight. I decided to show the film first and then have Jack speak to the team. Somewhere in the middle of the film, he appeared; stayed a few minutes; spoke briefly to Norm Nixon, who was sitting at the doorway; and left before the film ended. I asked Pat Riley to have Jack come in, but he was gone. I never found out exactly what happened to Jack. Did he get cold feet and shy away from addressing the team? Did he become alarmed that I had done things to the team differently in his absence? Or was it a case of bad timing? I never found out why he left, but I do know it was a rocky start.

After we returned from our next road trip, I saw Jack and suggested he do some scouting of opponents and ease himself back to work. He liked the opportunity but had some immediate problems. First, he couldn't yet travel by himself, so his wife, Claire, decided to go with him. He also couldn't write the report, because of his shattered elbow. And he couldn't fluently speak yet, so he was unable to deliver his observations to the team. But it was a start, and he courageously pursued it.

On a few occasions, Jack came to practice and delivered a scouting report to the team. His mind was as clever as ever. But his speech and memory had not caught up, and he would make mistakes and forget names and play sets.

The front-office people received Jack with open arms when he first appeared, but that quickly changed when they sensed that it was going to be a long time before he made a full recovery. Jack felt as though they were putting him off in allowing him back to his job. At one point, I heard he had some harsh words with Jerry West about taking his job away.

Just prior to the All-Star break, which was to be held at the Capitol Center in Landover, Maryland, our general manager, Bill Sharman, came to me and asked if I would speak with Jack about not rushing his return. Bill felt that I was the only one Jack would listen to. Jack wanted to attend the All-Star meeting and then take over the team, and Bill was asking me to explain why this couldn't be—that Jack wasn't ready. The agony of wanting him back and having to tell him not to come back, while at the same time running the team, was almost unbearable. I was trying to both encourage and caution him at the same time.

I left with the team for a two-game road trip en route to the All-Star break, and Jack was to meet us in Washington DC. The games were significant. We lost the first one to a weak Cleveland Cavalier team in a four-overtime marathon. Our players were frustrated and somewhat embarrassed to lose to the lowly Cavs. Norm Nixon and Kareem Abdul-Jabbar played over sixty minutes for nothing. The only humorous thing I remember about the game was that there were so many time-outs in the fourth quarter and subsequent four overtimes that I ran out of things to say. I lost my voice, and my lips were tired of repetition.

The next night, we had to play the rugged Chicago Bulls, and it would have been easy for our team to roll over. I held a special meeting and told them everyone in the country had read about the four-overtime game and that they were anxious to see how the Lakers would respond. Most people would expect a team to sulk and lose a few more, but a team with real style would come back sky high and rise above the disappointment. The team went out and played one of their finest games of the season. Our fast break was relentless. The Bulls didn't have a chance as we blew them out of their windy city. Sometimes games like this in midseason reveal what you will be like in the new season of the playoffs.

At the All-Star break, I met up with Jack and our wives for the three days of festivities. Although Jack was still behind in his speech recovery and memory, everything was fine. We all had a good time renewing friendships, and Jack got to see many people in the NBA who wished him the best and boosted his spirits. But then it was off to New York and back to work. No official decision had been made about his coaching status, so he was coming to New York and would attend practice sessions and games.

At practice it was awkward because I was directing the drills while Jack was on the court watching. It was difficult for both of us. I wanted him to take over, but it was very clear he simply was not ready. I was enjoying the coaching but also wanted Jack to have his job back. My frustration was immense but nothing in comparison to Jack's. He was so close to his team yet light-years away. I am sure he knew taking over the team was impossible at that time but also knew it was imperative he do so. The night of our game with the New York Knicks, Jack avoided coming to the game and instead went out to dinner with some friends from Philadelphia. The hurt was too much for him. He couldn't stand hanging around like an extra in a Broadway show, and so he left and went back to LA.

When we returned from our road trip, I met with Jack and sensed that things had gotten worse. In addition to his frustration in New York, he now felt as though he was being rebuffed by the front office. He got the impression that they were ignoring him, and that was exactly what he didn't need. Recovering from his head injury, Jack needed to rebuild his confidence, and his presence around the Lakers organization had produced the opposite. Jack realized he was not ready to handle the team, but he was totally frustrated with his superiors who were shelving him. Bill Sharman, Jerry West, and Jerry Buss were giving him the cold shoulder, and Jack thought it was because of something he had done.

I told him over lunch one day that I believed their attitude was not a result of things he had done wrong but that they were intentionally stalling because the team was doing so well without him. Even though I was the recipient of the Lakers organization's stall, I told Jack it was not because he was regressing in his recovery. At this moment, Jack was floundering and accepted my opinion. He was now going to ignore front-office rebuffs and continue to improve and wait a few more weeks.

I continued to give him scouting assignments, and he was doing much better. He traveled on his own and wrote out some of the material, and he was mentally sharp in his observations. There still were snags in his presentation to the team, with his stammering speech and forgetfulness, but it was getting better.

With six weeks to go in the season, Jack decided, ready or not, he must have the team back and went to Jerry Buss to reinstate him. Jack was told to wait. They were fearful he had not returned to full health for the rigors of the NBA and might harm himself by returning too soon, but deep down, their motivation was: Why make a coaching change with the team in first place and playing outstanding basketball?

I suspect that if the team had been struggling, they would have encouraged his return and advised getting back to work as the best therapy. Near the end of the season, Jerry Buss announced that Jack McKinney would not return as head coach for the entire year. This had been decided weeks before, but the announcement was delayed to see how the team was doing. Since we were going to win the Pacific Division, Jack had to wait until next year.

DURING THE SEASON, as acting head coach, I approached the Lakers about a salary adjustment. I was being paid $40,000 as an assistant coach but was performing as an interim head coach, an interim head coach guiding his team to a division title. I felt that a financial consideration should be made. The question of money was briefly mentioned during my first weeks as acting head coach. I told Jerry Buss I didn't want anything if it was going to hurt Jack McKinney, though I did hope they would award me a nice bonus for filling in.

Several weeks passed with me in my new position, and I heard nothing about a salary adjustment. I went to Bill Sharman, and he said not to worry, Jerry Buss was a very fair person who would deal with my position in a just manner. Again, after more weeks with no sign from Jerry Buss, I asked Sharman to request compensation. It was well into February when Sharman said Jerry Buss was willing to give me a $20,000 bonus. I was disappointed with his offer.

If Jerry Buss offered me $20,000 during the first month of my interim head coaching position, I would have gladly accepted. It would have been an encouraging gesture, and I would have been grateful. But Jerry Buss waited until my coaching skill was well established and then made an offer. I was upset with his proposed $20,000 raise and told Bill Sharman no thanks.

A few days later, Bill Sharman got back to me and said Jerry Buss was very upset with my rejection of the offer. He was not accustomed to making offers and having them turned down. I responded by saying I didn't think his offer was sufficient for the quality of work I was doing. After a few more weeks and continued success with the team, I finally met with Jerry Buss. He spent an hour telling me how he engineered the construction of this team over the summer and that my contribution to winning was nothing. I knew then, before we ever discussed dollars, that I was going to hold out for a full head coaching salary or accept nothing.

I couldn't believe I was being ripped apart by a man who should have been praising me for saving his team under difficult circumstances. Jerry Buss finally got to the money and said I could have anything I wanted, just subtract the amount from Jack McKinney's salary and playoff bonus and it was mine. He revealed to me he didn't feel any responsibility to pay Jack as a result of his injury and thus the money was mine for the asking. I couldn't believe the callousness of his remarks but also knew he saw the deep friendship between Jack and me. He was banking on me backing down to protect Jack, and that was exactly what happened.

I told Jerry Buss I didn't want a penny of Jack McKinney's money and would take zero if that was where my compensation was to come from. Jerry Buss then concluded by saying I could have the proposed $20,000 bonus with no strings attached. I told him then I wanted a full $120,000 salary for the season and not one cent of it to come from Jack McKinney or I wanted nothing. The meeting ended with no resolution, and I headed to the locker room to rouse up my team against Dr. J and the Sixers.

We played a great game in front of a sellout crowd and won decisively. Driving home that night, I evaluated the events of the day and promised myself I would not give in and accept Buss's offer. He was trying to exploit me, and I was going to make him pay for it, literally.

That decision eventually paid off for me. The Lakers pushed for me to accept the bonus since I was already under contract for two years. But I informed them that I had never actually *signed* my original contract because of a dispute concerning playoff money. Jack McKinney had offered me a half share of playoff money, but the wording in the contract was not clear. It read as only giving a half share if the team members didn't compensate me. This was not the same thing, and Jack had been working on it when he was injured. So the Lakers had one coach who was out with a serious injury and an interim coach who was working without a contract. Because of this technicality and my insistence for all or nothing, the Lakers finally gave me a full head coaching salary of $120,000, identical to Jack McKinney, who was to continue receiving his salary intact.

When this was finalized, I went to Jack McKinney and told him of my deal. I never told him of Buss's offer to pay me with his salary.

10

Looney Tunes

In the last month of the season, my intentions were to enjoy my new salary and look for a head coaching job elsewhere in the NBA. I hoped my record would be good enough to get a job no matter what happened in the upcoming playoffs. I anticipated Jack McKinney returning as head coach during the summer and running the team the following season. I had asked my personal friend and lawyer Richie Phillips to check around the league for opportunities. He told me of two possibilities: Dallas and San Antonio. I never actively pursued either job but did have a conversation with Bob Bass, the San Antonio general manager, and agreed to talk seriously about the position after the playoffs. My hope was to go far enough in the playoffs to cash in my interim Laker job for a permanent head coaching position with the Spurs.

During the playoffs, the question of how coaching shares were to be distributed was raised. The NBA sent a full share directly to the head coach, and in this case, Jerry Buss concluded that should be me. I objected to this, saying the original share should go to Jack McKinney and the Lakers should award me an additional share.

During this phase of negotiations, I found out that Jerry Buss had no intention of *ever* bringing Jack McKinney back. Through conversations with Richie Phillips, Buss stated his intentions were to go with someone else after the playoffs. He suggested that I may be a possibility along with some other names, principally Jerry Tarkanian from the University of Nevada, Las Vegas. I knew Buss was serious about Tarkanian, because he had already offered him the Lakers job, before hiring Jack McKinney, and Tarkanian had turned it down after his agent was mysteriously found dead in the trunk of his car.

During the Western Conference finals against Seattle, Tarkanian was the guest of Buss in his private box. It was our home opener, and we lost. Freddie Brown was drilling from downtown, and we couldn't contain his show. Afterward in the locker room, Buss alluded to what Tark said we should have done. I had the strong impression that discussions were going on then for Jerry Tarkanian to be the new Lakers coach. The only thing preventing it was if somehow we could keep on winning and go to the finals.

Jerry Buss had talked to Richie Phillips about the possibility of a deal for the future, but nothing was resolved. It appeared that Jerry Buss was going to wait until after the playoffs and then decide on his new coach.

I was in a quandary regarding what to tell Jack McKinney. We were in the middle of the playoffs, fighting for our lives, and here was Jack about to be dumped for good. If I told him of Buss's comments about not bringing him back, Buss would probably deny it and defer his decision until later. This confrontation would not help Jack, nor would it help me. It would probably open the door for Tarkanian the next year. Also, if I didn't tell Jack McKinney and we lost in the playoffs, Buss may reconsider keeping Jack, and I may have only one job opportunity, as assistant coach of the Lakers. I also calculated that since this was Jerry Buss's team and he hired Jack McKinney, he should be the one to tell him he was fired, not me. But none of these other options were satisfactory to me; I had to tell Jack what I knew.

During the championship series against the 76ers, Jack McKinney flew to Philadelphia to scout Games Three and Four. He was now much improved. His observations on how to contain Dr. J and other 76ers were insightful and accurate. We agreed to meet in the Philadelphia airport on our way home to LA and discuss the final games. He was not going back with the team but rather was going to Portland for a few days, to his old house, before coming home. While waiting for Jack in the airport, I called Richie Phillips, who had had a meeting that day with Jerry Buss. Richie told me that the meeting with Buss had been good and that he thought I would get an offer for the future. He cautioned me that nothing was definite, especially since we just lost to Philadelphia that afternoon and the series was now tied 2–2.

Just then, Jack McKinney showed up, and we spoke briefly about the game and what must be done about the future. As we talked, I made up my mind to tell him about Buss's apparent decision to fire him. But by then others traveling with the team had spotted us and come over to talk to Jack and wish him well. Our flight was boarding, so I resolved to tell Jack when we met up in LA in a few days. He was to be back home for Game Five in the Forum. It would be easier to tell him at home, but tell him I must, even if I blew it for myself.

I never got the opportunity to tell Jack, because the following day a syndicated article written by Frank Brady of the *Philadelphia Bulletin* appeared in an Oregon paper, stating that Jack McKinney was out for good. All the media in LA, as well as those covering the series nationally, went to Jerry Buss and asked if this is accurate. Buss responded, yes, it was true. Jack McKinney would not be hired back the next year. My chance to leak this information to Jack was over, and so was my close association with him.

Jack heard the news of his firing on the radio during his drive down the coast to LA. He then completely and totally disassociated himself with everything connected to the Lakers organization, myself included. I called Jack when he returned home, but he wanted no part of my conversation. Jack connected me with the events leading up to his dismissal. It had all happened too fast for him to swallow. He was fired, and soon after, I was hired permanently. I had fought for Jack throughout the season with Jerry Buss, and there was not a shadow of a doubt in my mind that I had been loyal to the man who had been so very good to me and my family. But somehow, it wasn't enough, and my friendship with Jack McKinney was a casualty, at least for the time being.

The NBA playoffs are a true test of a team's strength, and only the better team survives a seven-game series. It is a totally different experience from college and, for that matter, from the NBA regular season. We defeated the Phoenix Suns and then the Seattle Sonics to reach the NBA finals. The series against Philadelphia had a special significance for me. I had lived all my life in Philadelphia. I had learned to play basketball on the streets with other boys who had few alternatives for recreation other than the asphalt game of the city. This was where I had played college basketball at St. Joseph's, and this was where I had coached at La Salle College for the last nine years. My whole life had been Philadelphia basketball, and now I was challenging it for the world's championship.

Less than a year before, some Philadelphia basketball fans were scoffing at my fast break system, and now I was back, attacking the 76ers' system. It was out of a storybook that I would quietly leave my home in Philadelphia one September morning and arrive back in May with the best team in basketball, ready to play against Philadelphia's finest.

The regular-season game in Philadelphia was a blur to me. I spent the night before the game in Temple University Hospital with a kidney stone attack. I checked out of the hospital heavily drugged to ease the pain and came to the game. I hardly remember any of the contest except that Kareem was unstoppable, scoring 40 points, and Mike Cooper missed a finger-roll lay-up at the buzzer to lose by 1 point. I remember being in the locker room and surrounded by reporters asking me questions. I didn't know what they were saying. From the other end of the locker room, Kareem hollered out, "Hey, leave the man alone; he doesn't feel well." With that, they left and I collapsed.

That night we flew back to LA, and I went directly to Centinela Hospital. The surgeon made a quick appraisal. The kidney stone was lodged in the inner wall. It might have stayed that way for weeks, and I would have been sickly for the entire time. Or I could have immediate surgery and would be back on the job in four days. I wasn't too pleased about the operation, but losing weeks of coaching was out of the question. I agreed to the operation, and sure enough I was back coaching a game in four days.

After the game, I was wobbly but happy because we won. The doctor then took me aside and told me how they almost lost me during the operation. I stopped breathing for almost two minutes, until, at the prodding of the surgeon, the anesthesiologist got me going again, only after being threatened by the surgeon, "You better get him breathing, or we are going to make headlines on this one."

I look back now and think about how willingly I almost gave my life just so I could keep on coaching the Lakers and how callously it would eventually be taken away.

The finals opened in Los Angeles, because we had a better win percentage during the regular season. We gained that edge the last game of the season with a buzzer-beater at Golden State. Down by 1 point, with two seconds on the clock, Magic drove the lane and passed to Jim Chones for the winning basket. That win now gave us the important home-court advantage. If the series went the full seven games, the last game would be played in the Forum. We jumped on the 76ers in our home opener and beat them rather easily. The local press chided the ineffective play of Darryl Dawkins against Kareem Abdul-Jabbar. They changed his nickname from Chocolate Thunder to Chocolate Pudding. It was cute for them to say it, but we had only won the first game and had to deal with an angry Dawkins for the remaining games.

AFTER THE FIRST game of the Philadelphia series, we had a practice at Loyola Marymount University to go over some new strategy. In a team meeting before going on the court, Spencer Haywood fell into a deep sleep and was snoring loudly. We then proceeded to the court for our stretching ritual, much of which was performed lying on their backs. Spencer, who awakened to enter the court, proceeded to lie down and once again fall into a deep sleep. After fifteen minutes of different exercises, during which Spencer didn't move, we were ready to run full court.

Our trainer had to pull Spencer off to the side, and I directed him to go home. It was the next game that Spencer again worked the crowd to get himself into the game. The fans would chant, "We want Haywood!" which really started grinding on our team. After the game, I was sitting by myself in the training room, and Kareem walked over to me and simply said, "Get him out of here," and walked away.

I went up to Jerry Buss's office and delivered Kareem's comment and my concern. Dr. Buss suspended Spencer Haywood indefinitely. Spencer was removed from the team, never to return. However, after Kareem was injured in Game Five, while we were flying back to Philadelphia for Game Six, Jerry Buss sat with me and raised the question of who was going to replace Kareem. I told him I was going to start Magic Johnson at center. Dr. Buss loved Magic but wasn't convinced that this was the solution and suggested we bring Woody back from suspension to better fill Kareem's spot. On paper, Spencer Haywood was the best choice to replace Kareem, but I refused. I responded with an emphatic no, arguing that it would destroy our whole team, who had demonstrated their approval of Spencer's suspension. Seeing that I was adamant, Buss concluded by saying, "All right, you are the coach, and I'll honor your decision." But the reverse comment was also planted: "If we lose the championship, I will hold you responsible."

Sure enough, in Game Two Darryl Dawkins had destroyed us with outside jumpers and inside power moves. No one had dared get in his way that night. The 76ers built a sizable lead going into that fourth quarter, but we came back and tied the game with less than a minute to go. At a time out, I glanced at the 76ers and could see the look of defeat in their eyes. They couldn't believe after playing so well against us that we were even. The 76ers got a break and won that game with a desperation shot by Bobby Jones. They enjoyed the moment of victory, but they knew what I knew—that we were the better team and we would win the series. After this loss, I was more confident we could win the championship than I was after our first win.

We then went to Philly for Game Three and had to win one game there to even the home-court advantage. Spencer Haywood had been suspended; however, the team was playing above the problem. Kareem was unstoppable inside, and we beat the 76ers in the Spectrum. It was the Lakers' first win in Philadelphia for a long time, and it sure felt good to do it in my hometown.

That night, Pat Riley and I went to study the videotape of the game and found we had recorded the wrong channel; it was Bugs Bunny and Looney Tunes, not the 76ers and Lakers. I called a friend, Al Meltzer, a local TV sports announcer, and asked if we could come over and see the game tapes. He agreed, so we went to the studio and studied the film well into the night. It didn't matter in Game Four; the 76ers were destined to win.

We played well but got no breaks in the game. Kareem was being mugged under our basket, and he didn't go to the foul line the whole game. For the first time in the series, I was worried. We played so well and lost. Maybe the momentum had swung and the 76ers were on a roll.

Game Five was back in Los Angeles, and we had to win to break the tie at 2–2. The pressure was now on us, since the 76ers could expect to go home and win the next game. For most of the game, the 76ers were outplaying us. They were playing with much more confidence, and we were struggling to stay within 10 points of their lead. It was late in the third quarter when Kareem made a skyhook and cut the lead to 8 points but turned and crumbled to the floor. He was carried off the court, possibly taking with him our hopes of winning the championship.

With our team of greyhounds—Nixon, Cooper, Wilkes, and Magic—we scrambled back and took the lead going into the fourth quarter. Surely this would not last with the inside power of the 76ers. As we started the last period, Kareem came back on the floor in pain and heavily taped. He was ready to do whatever it took to win the game. He knew he was the star and that this was the time for his performance. There could be no delay. The curtain was up. Kareem equalized the 76ers' inside game, and going down to the wire, the score was even.

We called a time-out and set up our No. 45 play, which meant the ball handler would take it to Kareem's side and fake a pass to him, drawing the defense over. After the fake, the ball would be swung high to Magic, who would deliver the ball to Kareem rolling across the lane. The play worked to perfection. Norm Nixon took the ball to Kareem's side, and on the fake pass, Darryl Dawkins closed out the passing lane, insuring no pass to Kareem on his side. Nixon then passed to Magic, who made a perfect lead pass to Kareem's open side. Just as the ball was about to sail out of bounds, Kareem dragged his leg across the lane and snared the ball in between Dawkins and Julius Erving. He broke through the double-team defense and scored the basket. He then went to the foul line and, on one leg, lifted the ball through the net for a game-winning three-point play.

Kareem had lived up to the script. The star must deliver the points at the crucial moment. Kareem knew the whole season came down to his ability on that play, and he did it. The joy of going ahead 3–2 in the series was short lived when Kareem was whisked away to the hospital for X-rays. At least for that night we were in the lead.

At the airport the following day we found out Kareem was not coming to Philadelphia. He had a badly sprained ankle. While he could possibly play Game Seven back in Los Angeles, he would definitely not make Game Six in Philadelphia. My wife, Cassie, decided to come with us anyway. She wanted to make sure we wouldn't win the championship without her. She grinned, and we both knew what we were thinking—that we were going to win at home in Philadelphia.

The team boarded the plane in disbelief, hoping to see the captain of our team flop into his favorite front seat. But as we took off, Kareem was missing, and Magic Johnson was in his seat. I was sure Magic did it on purpose to announce to those who knew the significance, "I am in *the man*'s seat, and I will take his place in the game." Symbolically, Magic was taking over as the star of the team and had already moved into his dressing room.

It was during this flight that I decided to start Magic at center. Although he was our point guard, Magic was a natural for the spot. He was six feet nine and strong. He could outquick Darryl Dawkins inside and run around him outside. At our shootaround the day of Game Six, we were very loose. We had fun going over play sets with Magic at center. He was learning them for the first time, and the players enjoyed his mistakes. Magic, however, was happy with his new position. He played center in high school and liked the challenge.

My plan was to start him at center and then move him around to guard and forward to frustrate the 76ers' defensive assignments. We left the practice session ready for a fun night. We were giggling like a group of schoolkids going on a trip to Disneyland. Someone was going to have a good time in the Spectrum that night, and we knew it was going to be us.

WHEN WE ARRIVED for the game, we heard loud banging noises near the dressing rooms. It was a group of carpenters frantically constructing a platform for a potential championship ceremony. No one in their right mind expected us to win, but it was a league rule to be ready if mathematically the series could end. To the 76ers, the platform must have looked like a guillotine being made ready for an execution. To them, the hammering was a piercing sound of danger; their heads could roll this very night.

For the introductions, I informed the public address announcer that Magic Johnson would play center. I wanted the world to know Magic was the man for this game. In our team huddle before the start of the game, Jim Chones said, "Okay, I'm jumping center for Kareem, right?" I answer, "No, Jim, as we practiced, Magic is Kareem tonight."

The opening tip went to us, and we proceeded to run our first play to Magic down in the low post. This had always been a play called only for Kareem, but not tonight. Magic received the pass and wheeled around with a skyhook . . . nothing but net.

We jump out to an early lead with Magic Johnson doing it all—scoring inside with skyhooks and outside as our point guard on the fast break. The 76ers didn't know whom to put on Magic; sometimes it should have been Darryl Dawkins, while other times it should have been Maurice Cheeks. On the downside, we were not getting any scoring from our two shooters, Norm Nixon and Jamaal Wilkes. If they didn't get hot, we were in trouble. Also, the game was being officiated by two local referees, Jack Madden and Joe Gushue. Madden had since moved down south, but Gushue had a reputation of being nice to the local team. I was determined to jump all over Joe Gushue early in the game to accentuate his Philly reputation. As expected, the first few calls by Gushue went to the 76ers, and I was screaming at him. Then he called a three-second violation against the 76ers. I jumped up and yelled to Jack Madden that Joe Gushue made a mistake; he thought we were on offense. Madden and Gushue laughed at my sarcasm, and by the second quarter, my message was received by the officials. They proceeded to call a very fair, impartial game.

At halftime we were up 2 points. I told the team we were in great shape. The 76ers were shooting over 60 percent, and our best shooters were practically scoreless. Both items had to change in the second half to our benefit. I told Nixon and Wilkes to keep shooting despite their misses. The team was excited about the second half; they were not afraid the 76ers would crush them at any moment.

During the second half the 76ers made a strong comeback and almost caught us. Jamaal Wilkes was keeping our lead with an unstoppable array of shots. Every time the 76ers got close, Jamaal scored another hoop. He wound up with 37 points, all but 5 in the second half. Magic continued to do his thing of following missed shots and making key foul shots. He made a perfect 14 for 14 from the free-throw line en route to a 42-point performance. His effort was so spectacular that they erased Kareem's name from being selected most valuable player of the series and inserted Magic Johnson for this singular great achievement.

The shot that sealed our victory, however, came from Jim Chones. Up to this game, Chones was having a rocky playoff season. During much of the Phoenix series and then into the Seattle set, Chones was unproductive. We were winning in spite of him or with him on the bench and Mike Cooper in his place. But in the 76ers series, he loosened up a bit, and in the clinching game, he was at his best. He did a terrific job on the boards and made some key defensive blocks. Now with our lead cut to a few points and the 24-second clock running down, Jim Chones took a turnaround jump shot that we desperately needed to go in. The shot was a brick. It clanged off the front rim and ricocheted ten feet in the air and then miraculously fell into our basket. The day was saved by Jim Chones, and for his effort that evening, he deserved a break.

Just after Chones's two-point brick, the Philly fans knew it was over. They became restless and began to boo their team, who had played so well and had come so far. It makes you wonder about fans who will jeer their players during a World Series. With all that noise, I looked up at the clock and realized with less than two minutes to play we were ahead for keeps. That moment of awareness reserved for special occasions hit me. I turned to Pat Riley and exclaimed, "We are gonna win the world championship!" Prior to that instant, I was too involved in the game and making coaching adjustments, to ponder the significance of the game. This was probably true of the entire team. They just worked so hard at compensating for the absence of our dominating center that they never thought about the importance of the contest. With seconds remaining, Jim Chones threw the ball to the roof, and the players embraced one another in an act of total joy. The feeling of happiness was so complete that time seemed to stop. We were existing in another world. This exhilaration lasted only a few moments, but I remembered it for many years. Quickly, Spectrum guards grabbed us and escorted the team to the championship ceremony.

The championship trophy was presented by Commissioner Larry O'Brien on that new platform we witnessed being constructed prior to the game. I wondered if it would hold us, since no one really thought it would be used. The commissioner presented the trophy to our team owner, Jerry Buss, who didn't seem ready for the national TV exposure. I know he was a casual dresser, but his tattered jeans outfit revealed that he, too, expected the ceremony another night. The players on stage—Magic, Norm, and Jamaal—all thanked their teammates, especially Kareem, who was back home watching the festivities on TV. I added a well-deserved thank you to Jack McKinney, who laid the foundation for this achievement. The thrill of accepting the championship award could not match the final moments on the court.

To my surprise, when we arrived back in our dressing room, the players were quiet. Sure, there were people yelling and screaming and pouring champagne on one another, but the players were subdued. They were physically and emotionally exhausted. The joy of winning makes all the hand slapping and champagne spilling seem small and insignificant. We all went back to the hotel for a celebration with a small group of friends who made this predictably uneventful trip.

During the game, Cassie was at the Spectrum all by herself surrounded by Philadelphia 76ers fans. The fans sensed that she was for the Lakers and ignored her occasional cheer. With a minute to go, they realized Cassie was my wife, and they stood around her and applauded our Lakers victory. Sometimes Philadelphia fans can be kind. Little did the crowd know that both of us were born and raised in the City of Brotherly Love. Most of our loyal followers were back in LA, waiting for Game Seven. Some writers for newspapers in the east pulled a cute trick by staying in LA a few extra days and waiting for Game Seven to come back to them. I would love to see the personal touch they gave in their accounts of the championship game.

The flight back to LA the next morning was like the locker room, quiet and reserved. The team was savoring the victory with a childlike grin rather than a boisterous laugh. As soon as we touched down in LA, Kareem was brought on board and was engulfed by our players. They knew he was the one who got them to Game Six. They knew he was the star who carried them through crucial moments all season long. They knew he was *the man*. With Kareem on board, the team was again full of life. Now that everyone was present, the celebration started in earnest.

We were taken from the plane in limousines to the Forum for a welcome reception by the fans. My children were also brought to the Forum from our Palos Verdes home by limo. They told me later that day that they wanted a limo all the time from then on. My five-year-old daughter, Juliet, thought it was great to watch TV in the back seat and stop at McDonald's on the way to the parade.

The reception by the fans was an exciting new experience. Thousands of people gathered to thank us for bringing joy to their city. They were proud to live in Los Angeles because of our achievement.

The following day, we had our final team meeting during a cocktail reception for all the Forum employees. This was when the players voted for playoff shares. I stressed with them to be fair in their decisions and not let money tarnish their achievement. Since I expected to receive a full share from Jerry Buss, I told them that I was covered and to consider others in the organization. I thanked them for their efforts and left them alone to decide on business. The results clearly showed their generosity. The team voted for full shares totaling over $30,000 each to Pat Riley and Jack Curran. They also awarded a full share to Butch Lee, who was with us less than half a season and never got off the bench.

But their generosity stopped with Spencer Haywood. He had been with the team for the entire season, except for the last four games of the Philly series, and they voted him a quarter share. It was the players showing their displeasure with Haywood's selfish actions during our crucial struggle. The team wanted their disapproval of Spencer Haywood to go on public record. It was the strongest reprimand players could inflict on a teammate. The question of Spencer Haywood returning to the Lakers next year was decided in that meeting. He was not welcome.

To tie a bow on the Spencer Haywood saga, he wasn't welcome not only on the Lakers but on any other NBA team and ended up playing briefly in Europe. The following season, he was signed by the Washington Bullets, whom the Lakers happened to be playing early in the season. Going out to the court, I was fearful of what might happen when Spencer saw me, thinking he believed me to be the man who ruined his NBA career.

Both teams were warming up, and I stayed down at the Lakers basket, glancing down to spot Haywood. He saw me and broke out of the lay-up line and came running right at me. I thought of running the other way but was pretty much stuck.

Spencer came up to me, put his arms out, and wrapped me up. "Coach, it's good to see you!"

I was speechless. Spencer was over his anger and bitterness; he had moved on. I finally said, "Good seeing you, Woody." That was the last time I saw Spencer Haywood for several years, until he came to my office at Loyola Marymount to apologize for attempting to have me killed. Spencer had come a long way from his stupor on the basketball floor, coincidentally, at Loyola Marymount.

The day after the championship game in Philadelphia, Richie Phillips met with Jerry Buss and negotiated a contract. Buss agreed to hire me as head coach, but the salary and number of years were undetermined. I wanted the joy of this championship success to continue next year. However, I recognized my options. I could leave and go to San Antonio. It certainly would reduce the hurt between Jack McKinney and me. My deeper feelings, however, reminded me I never betrayed Jack, so turning down the Lakers job now would only hurt me.

I resolved to be demanding in negotiations with the Lakers. I did not trust the organization, because of what they did to Jack McKinney. If they were capable of running him out of town for falling off a bicycle, they were capable of doing it to me. I told Richie Phillips to construct a large payout over three years, and if Jerry Buss wouldn't accept, then I would leave. I realized I was, perhaps for the last time, in the driver's seat. With the recent firing of Jack McKinney and our championship performance, Jerry Buss needed me to make it all fit. Hiring me would make Buss look like a genius who masterminded the whole championship sequence, and losing me would raise serious doubts about Jerry Buss and his dealings.

The next day, we were taken on a parade through the city. I had spent a year in Los Angeles, and this was my first time downtown. My new life in the NBA consisted of the Forum, LAX, and Palos Verdes. All three spots are a good distance from the center of town. In our open cars, we were touched by thousands who came out to see the team. They reached out to touch us and be a part of the victory. The parade ended with a reception at City Hall, but because the crowds were too large, we were brought into Mayor Tom Bradley's office for safekeeping.

During the delay, Magic Johnson came over to Jerry Buss and said in front of me, "What are you going to do with Coach Westhead? If you don't keep him, then I'll go wherever he's coaching." At this moment, Magic's words were golden, since the terms of my proposed contract had not been resolved. With his comment, I suspect they just went up. Of course, the inescapable irony was that Magic Johnson would be the very player whose comments would get me fired a year and a half later.

The City Hall ceremony was moved to the rooftop for security reasons. As we stood well above the massive crowd, hearing their cheers of approval, it reminded me of Jesus on the mountaintop being tempted by Satan. I was full of happiness and yet wondered if I might fall into ruin. Would all the glory and new money dash me to the ground? Would I get caught up in life in the fast lane and forget my roots? I hoped not.

Our last team function before we split for the summer, and some of us split forever, was a private dinner Jerry Buss hosted just for the team. He wanted to wrap things up and set the stage for the future. One of the items was announcing the coach for next season. We had gotten close to an agreement, but it was not definite. Richie Phillips met again that afternoon with Jerry Buss, but there had been no official agreement. Richie Phillips was insisting the terms read that I would be head coach for three years, in accordance with NBA standards. He was eliminating the possibility of a capricious firing without full compensation. The lawyers were fighting over this issue as the team dinner was going on. During the coffee and dessert, Richie called me and said we had no deal. Just then, Jerry Buss got up and announced to the team I would be their coach next season. I couldn't ruin the party, so I just sat and smiled.

The next day, there was to be a press conference to announce my signing, but fifteen minutes before the scheduled time, we were still in disagreement. Jerry Buss finally submitted and accepted our terms. We met the media as if the deal had been settled for days. Jerry Buss announced me as the Lakers coach for the next three years. He proclaimed that I was the best and wealthiest coach in the country.

The days immediately following the championship and my new contract were like a daydream. I went on vacation for a few days to Palm Springs with my wife, but I was in a daze. It was as if there was a film between me and the world. I was on such an emotional high that it was hard to get back in touch with things. We came home and went to a Dodgers game for relaxation, and I was swarmed by fans who recognized me in public. This was the first time I had ever felt like a public figure; I think I liked it.

I think.

11

The Glitter Is Gone

Now is the winter of our discontent.
—WILLIAM SHAKESPEARE, *Richard III*

My first function as permanent head coach was to attend the annual NBA meetings being held in Los Angeles. What a coincidence they were scheduled here in 1980 and in Boston the following year, which was to be the home of the new champions. At the meetings there was a distinct feeling of distance between me and my fellow coaches. Some of them were treating me like a new kid on the street who hadn't been properly initiated into the fraternity.

Cotton Fitzsimmons and I nearly came to blows during the season over this matter. We were in Kansas City, and just near the end of the first half, the Kings scored a basket. I objected to the officials that time had run out. Cotton came storming over and demanded the officials get me out of there since I didn't know the rules. I then turned and charged Cotton Fitzsimmons. I replied I had a right to question the clock and told him to mind his own business. The guards held us back, and the matter ended. From that day forward Cotton Fitzsimmons was friendly toward me, as if I had met his challenge of initiation and passed the course.

Well, for others, I still hadn't passed. They saw me as a lucky college coach who came into the league and won the world championship, while they had labored many years and still searched for the golden ring. The others, I suspect, were angry with me for what had happened to Jack McKinney. They assumed I was involved in his exit. This really hurt me because in college I was always well liked by my colleagues as someone considerate of others. Now I was the robber baron from out west. Fortunately, my college coach, Jack Ramsay, who was president of the NBA Coaches Association, welcomed me as an old friend. He knew more about the scene with Jack McKinney and me than most others and seemed to accept my role.

Of course, my first and really only concern was my team and defending our title. Our first step toward that would be through the upcoming college draft. We had a weak bench, and with Spencer Haywood indefinitely suspended, we needed some help to maintain our dominance. I knew absolutely nothing about the college players. The season had been so confusing with our reshuffling of coaching positions that all the college scouting had been done by Jerry West.

He picked Wayne Robinson from Virginia Tech, in the second round, as our first choice. This was the start of my conflict with Jerry West. After a few days of training camp, I decided I didn't like Wayne Robinson's game and quickly dispatched him to the Detroit Pistons for a second-round pick in 1981. I meant no malice toward West; I just thought Robinson could not help our team.

Unfortunately, West felt as though I was attempting to expose his work. I had thwarted his expert judgment. To Jerry West the only logical conclusion was, since he was right about Wayne Robinson, I must have been incompetent.

In an attempt to avoid being caught short of firsthand information for next year's draft, I pushed for a second assistant coach who would spend all his time scouting both pro teams and college players. In that way, I would have necessary information to supplement the Jerry West system. I narrowed the field down to two: Joe O'Connor, my former assistant at LaSalle College, and Mike Thibault, a scout from the Seattle area who worked part time for us this past season. Jerry West suggested a friend of his back in West Virginia, but clearly this pick must be my choice. I finally select Mike Thibault because of his NBA experience. My pick was not popular with Jerry West, who proceeded for the ensuing year to criticize the activity of Thibault. I knew this was another problem between West and I, but I felt that as long as we did well, I could withstand his criticism.

AS WE OFFICIALLY opened training camp in Palm Springs, I was aware no one had repeated as champions in twelve years. I had the feeling we would break the streak and win again that year, but ponder the lesson of history. Something must happen to a team that impedes their continued success. Well, within the next ten months I would find out all about those hidden secrets.

My opening address to the team was an analysis of what we must do to win. Basically, that meant each player must be content to play the same role as last season. I cautioned that we could not allow the glory of winning the championship to change our working habits. I told them, for example, Magic could not say he'd had enough of rebounding in the lane and was now going to strictly be an outside shooter, and Mike Cooper could not say, "The heck with tough, hard-nosed defense like I put on Dr. J. I want my points." The key was to sharpen their skills following the same rules for our team. I also announced a new, improved fast break system that would get us more opportunities but would demand more hard work.

As we opened practice, problems immediately began to surface. Kareem, our leader, was horribly out of shape. He hadn't played since his ankle injury several months ago and was struggling to get up and down the court. Jim Chones, in contrast, was in super condition, as he should have been, and wanted to prove his ability. Kareem and Chones finally came to blows during a scrimmage, and all our embracing friendship was out the window.

It was Magic who separated Kareem and Chones and who demanded that they stop fighting and play basketball. Magic Johnson was off to a strong start in practice and was in the process of taking over the team. He was flexing his muscles as the new leader.

Also causing considerable friction was my new fast break system. The system demanded that each player sprint to a designated spot on the court on every offensive possession. All five players were going full speed with the ball either from a steal, a defensive rebound, or a made basket by the opposition. There was no downtime to catch your breath. But our players were already showing the symptoms of why teams don't repeat as champions; they want to get by with less work than it took to win the title. Too much success had spoiled the fast break because it is too demanding for champions. For the remainder of training camp, there existed unhappiness among the players. I wanted them to be whistling while they worked. They wound up bickering while they went through the motions.

During the exhibition season, things got worse. I sensed that Magic Johnson was going too far in his new role as team leader. He was being gruff and abrupt to other players when they made mistakes. He was pleased only when things went his way. He didn't want any advice from me. He was falling into the perfect mold of a know-it-all. I decided before our opening game to talk to him and tell him my observations. I reminded him of the case of Dennis Johnson, who, like Magic, was voted MVP in the championship series the year before and who the following year brought ruin to the Sonics. DJ was so incompatible with his teammates that Seattle traded him away after the season. I cautioned Magic that the signs of this were there for him. He assured me I was wrong, and we let the matter go.

To no one's surprise, we started the season sluggish and out of sync. We opened in Seattle and got lucky at the end on a steal by Mike Cooper and a basket at the buzzer. We didn't deserve to win, and Seattle, who had waited all summer to get back at us, did deserve the victory but nonetheless lost.

We came home for our Forum opener against the Houston Rockets. Before the game, Commissioner O'Brien presented our championship rings. It was a proud moment to stand in front of our fans and receive rings symbolizing the best basketball team in the world. It brought me back to those fleeting moments in Philadelphia the previous May when we won the title. I couldn't believe I went from struggling to get mediocre players as a small college coach to coaching the finest players in the world to a championship. As it had for F. Scott Fitzgerald's character Jay Gatsby, an impossible dream came true. I reached out and found the green light of my dreams, but it had already begun to fade. The joy ride was over and the grind was upon us.

Just before the game, they lowered the championship banner from the rooftop. I looked around and saw many more open spaces and wondered how many we would fill. After all the festivities, the game seemed unimportant. We won the contest but lost Kareem due to an eye injury. He was slapped in the face by Rudy Tomjanovich on a rebound attempt. Kareem was furious, for it wasn't the first time his eyes were damaged. It was also somewhat darkly fitting that Tomjanovich, who a few years before almost lost his life when he was punched in the face by the Lakers' Kermit Washington in the Forum, now delivered an accidental blow to Kareem.

The injury was not serious, but Kareem was unable to play for a week. The layoff really hurt Kareem because he was just getting back into playing form after a sluggish exhibition season. The delay set him back a few more weeks into the season. When he returned to action, Kareem was wearing his old goggles of two years ago. He never wore them during the championship season, and I didn't like the equipment switch. I confronted Jack Curran, our trainer, who he said Kareem was worried about permanent eye injury and wouldn't play without them, so on went the blinkers.

We won our first five games but were not playing well. Then we dropped two games at home against San Antonio and Denver. The real world had arrived. I met with the team and explained what was happening. Teams were playing full throttle against us for forty-eight minutes. Even when we had an 8-point lead in the last quarter, as we had gotten against Denver, teams weren't rolling over. They kept coming at us now because we were special. We were the world champions, and it would make their season to nail us. The players began to see the new challenge. It would take us a while yet to come out ready for a war in every city.

THE PLAYERS SUGGESTED we get more movement in our set offense. They felt as though we were going inside to Kareem too much. I suggested they could always correct this by running the fast break more and getting open shots ahead of Kareem. But to show I respected their concerns, I also added a few wrinkles to the offense for new guard-forward opportunities. Magic was trying to exert his influence and control the tempo of the game to his liking. I could see trouble ahead. He had gotten too much, too soon.

We had a monster on our hands, and someone was going to get hurt. I remember a remark made to me by my La Salle College assistant, Joe O'Connor, about a flashy freshman who by midseason was telling all the seniors where to play. O'Connor turned to me and calmly said, "Methinks, Dr. Frankenstein, there's been a slight miscalculation." We were on a collision course with Magic Johnson.

A few games later, in Atlanta, Magic was tackled by Tom Burleson going for a loose ball and got up mighty slow. Magic's leg was sore, but he continued to play. During the next week at practice, I decided to chew him out for acting like a pampered star, but he competed so hard in a scrimmage that I changed my mind. I went over and patted him on the back. I encouraged him rather than reprimanded him. Perhaps a spoonful of sugar would turn him around. The next day, he came to our shootaround and said he could hardly walk. He sat and watched our warm-up for Kansas City that night. Magic tried to play but collapsed in the first quarter. He had torn cartilage in his knee and needed immediate surgery.

I'll never forget visiting him in the hospital the day of his operation. He was in the same room in Centinela Hospital as I had been when I had my kidney stone removed. Incidentally, Magic Johnson and Kareem Abdul-Jabbar were the only two players on the team to visit me in the hospital. I wanted to return the courtesy to Magic and to see how he would be a few hours after surgery. I walked into his room expecting to see him moaning and groaning in pain but found him sitting up, eating apple pie, and watching the Rams game with his Dodger blue hat on and a big grin.

I felt sorry for Magic because he loved the game so much. Yet I saw the injury as a blessing in disguise. I couldn't stop his collision course of the star syndrome, but the knife did. He would be lost to us for forty-five games and, during that time, would come back to earth. His leg may never be as good, but his mind would be healed.

With Magic gone, we had to come up with a new act. We were the world champion LA Lakers without our Magic show. There were several areas critically weakened by his absence. We were now very thin at guard. Norm Nixon was the only other player capable of handling the ball and running the team. Mike Cooper was developing nicely but not as a ball handler.

Also, our rebounding was seriously weakened. We would miss Magic's great second effort on the offensive boards. And finally, we would sorely miss him at the end of a game, when Magic became a savant.

Under these difficult circumstances, we went on a five-game losing streak. We just couldn't get the right combination to sustain winning. Our opponents were stalking us like a wounded deer; they smelled blood and were on the hunt. I decided to shake up the starting lineup to change our luck, so I moved Jim Chones and Mike Cooper out of the lineup and brought Jim Brewer and Butch Carter up.

I announced to the media that this would be my new balance-of-energy policy to get a better mix of talent on the court throughout the game. Mike Cooper responded well. He was more relaxed as a substitute and played better in his new role. Jim Chones vehemently resisted the switch. He screamed to the press that he was being singled out as the problem, while the real one was being overlooked—namely, the mediocre play of Kareem. There were anonymous comments in the papers by Lakers players blaming Kareem for our weakness.

I couldn't believe the switch in allegiance. Kareem Abdul-Jabbar was the greatest player in all of basketball and had just led us to a world championship, and now players wanted to cut his throat. I threatened the team that I would not tolerate nameless comments to the press about our team. If you couldn't put your name next to the criticism, then keep quiet. Otherwise, I was going to run you out of town. There was never any conclusive evidence of who was making the derogatory comments about Kareem's play, but I believed all indications pointed to Chones and Norm Nixon. I am sure Kareem had a good idea of who it was, even though he acted as if it didn't bother him. He was such a sensitive person; I am sure he was seething inside.

At the very moment we seemed to be falling completely apart, we started winning. We went on a five-game winning streak, and the balance of energy looked like a stroke of genius. Kareem had moved into high gear since Magic's injury and was now destroying everything in sight. Jamaal Wilkes was enjoying his best offensive season of his career. We were running some new plays for him, and he was getting close to 30 points a game. Norm

Nixon was playing well enough; he was a tough competitor. But his knees were ailing, and he was still complaining about my emphasis on Kareem. So was Jim Chones, who was still dragging his feet. He was sulking on the court and acted as if he hoped we would lose. The total picture was that we were playing outstanding basketball. We had adjusted to life without Magic Johnson and had discovered what we needed to do to win, and we were doing it.

THOUGH I BELIEVED it was imperative for us to trade Jim Chones, it was Nixon who attracted interest from other teams. The Denver Nuggets offered to trade David Thompson for Norm Nixon. Our general manager, Bill Sharman, was very excited about the deal. He believed Thompson would help our scoring and rebounding power. Jerry Buss liked the idea because David Thompson represented one of a select group of superstars who excite the fans by his mere presence on the floor. At his best, David Thompson has been seen leaping tall buildings en route to a spectacular slam dunk.

For these reasons, the Lakers organization wanted to do the deal. I was reluctant and put them off by demanding we find out more about Thompson's physical health before we did anything. Jerry West was sent to Denver to see Thompson play and gather information on his readiness. Jerry West reported back that David Thompson was scoring almost at will and that his health seemed to be fine. I decided to go scout David Thompson in person to evaluate the pending trade. On a free day, Pat Riley and I flew to Seattle to see Thompson play against the Sonics. We didn't want to make it an official trip, so we got to the Kingdome and bought tickets from scalpers outside the arena. With trench coats on, we sat high up behind the basket. No one recognized me, but the people behind us recognized Riley. Our collective opinion after watching the game was that David Thompson was not a fit for the Lakers. He played okay against Seattle but wasn't the guard we needed. The deal was all but complete, except I still disagreed. I sensed the others were annoyed with my dissent. But I had some strong doubts, so I said no.

A major concern was who would handle the ball, especially on the fast break, without Nixon and with Magic injured. I felt that Norm Nixon was a key to our offensive flow and that David Thompson would not provide that valuable element. The Lakers management argued that this would only be a temporary problem and that with the return of Magic Johnson, we would have the biggest and best backcourt in the game. I conceded that things would be much improved with Magic handling the ball, but I was not convinced that David Thompson would be better than Nixon as a sidekick for Magic Johnson.

In one respect, I should have consented to the deal because Norm Nixon had been fighting me every inch of the way. He was outspoken in his disapproval of my handling of Jim Chones. Norm Nixon was a malcontent who never missed an opportunity to knock me and my plan of attack. Now I had the perfect opportunity to send him off to Denver and be rid of him. But Nixon always gave a good hard effort on the court, even if he hated your guts, which was fine with me. I could put up with his grumbling as long as he did his job.

Consequently, because I believed Nixon would help us win more than David Thompson, I stopped the trade. Jerry Buss, seeing a split decision between me and the rest of the front office, decided to consult Magic Johnson, who was back in Lansing, Michigan, recuperating at home. I thought it dangerous to bring Magic into a matter concerning a fellow teammate, but Buss believed Magic would know who would blend in best with him. Magic's answer was trade Nixon. Magic Johnson preferred playing with David Thompson in the backcourt. It would allow him to handle the ball all the time, versus sharing the ball with Nixon.

With Magic Johnson's input, we had one final meeting to decide on the trade, and again I voted against it. The matter was dropped, and we kept our backcourt intact. I must admit it annoyed me a great deal to see Norm Nixon complaining about how I mishandled him and the team, while, behind closed doors, I was fighting for his career with the Lakers.

IN EARLY FEBRUARY, Magic Johnson started practicing on his own and traveling with the team. It was good to have him back. He was the best cheerleader a team could ever have. We started working him with our second team after the regular practice, and it really helped his progress. He could finally go all out in practice and seemed fit and ready for games. Jerry Buss decided to delay his starting date a couple of weeks beyond when the doctors said he was ready. He reasoned that Magic was so valuable, why rush it? I disagreed with Buss upstaging the professional evaluations of the doctors who said he could play as well as the coaches who had seen him in practice every day, but I didn't try to change Buss's mind, because the team was playing great basketball. We had won twenty-eight games in Magic's forty-five-game absence, and I didn't think anyone could have done any better. I felt I did a better job in my second year with the Lakers than I had in the first, when we won it all. But success in Los Angeles is measured in championships, so this achievement without Magic would go unnoticed.

1. Paul Westhead with Pat Riley on the Los Angeles Lakers, 1980. Scott Cunningham / National Basketball Association via Getty Images.

2. St. Joseph's University basketball team, 1959–60. Paul Westhead pictured fourth from left, number 32. Saint Joseph's University Athletics.

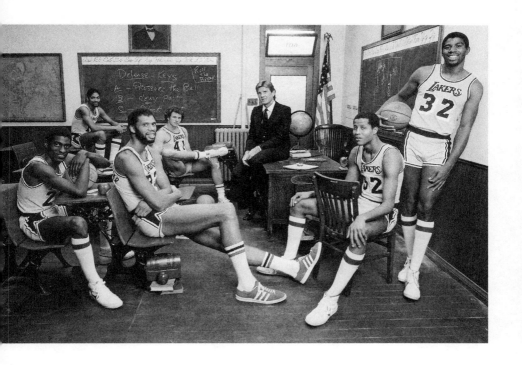

3. Los Angeles Lakers classroom scene with Magic Johnson, Jamal Wilkes, Kareem Abdul-Jabbar, Michael Cooper, Norm Nixon, and Mitch Kupchak, 1980. Lane Stewart / Sports Illustrated Classic via Getty Images.

4. Hank Gathers and Bo Kimble, Loyola Marymount University, 1989. Associated Press.

5. Paul Westhead after taking over as head coach of the Lakers in 1980. Associated Press.

6. Paul Westhead coaching the Denver Nuggets, 1991. Stephen Dunn / Getty Images Sport.

7. Dwight Howard and Paul Westhead, Orlando Magic, 2004. Fernando Medina / National Basketball Association via Getty Images.

8. Paul Westhead talking to Luke Ridnour with the Seattle SuperSonics, 2008. Jesse D. Garrabrant / National Basketball Association via Getty Images.

9. Pat Riley, Paul Westhead, Kareem Abdul-Jabbar, and Magic Johnson with the Lakers, 1980. Manny Millan / Sports Illustrated via Getty Images.

10. Paul Westhead coaching a practice with the Lakers in 1980. Peter Read Miller / Sports Illustrated via Getty Images.

11. Paul Westhead coaching the Nuggets with assistant coach Jim Boyle, 1991. NBA Photos / National Basketball Association via Getty Images.

12. Paul Westhead next to Eddie Jordan and Magic Johnson during the Lakers' 1981–82 season. Focus on Sport / Getty Images Sport.

13. Paul Westhead with Magic Johnson getting his MVP Award after the 1980 season. Associated Press.

14. Paul Westhead with his wife, Cassie Westhead, and his mother, Jane Westhead. Courtesy of the author.

15. Paul Westhead raising the WNBA Championship Trophy with Diana Taurasi and the Phoenix Mercury in 2007. Associated Press.

12

The Wrong Star

Magic Johnson returned against the New Jersey Nets in the Forum and was reintroduced to the media in true Hollywood style. During our pregame warm-ups, there was a picture-taking ceremony conducted by *Sports Illustrated*. Everything stopped as Magic posed with his arms spread like a returning conqueror. We won the game, and Magic's debut was well received by the fans, though not by his teammates. There was an immediate resentment toward Magic stealing the show after the team had worked so hard and so well without him. Norm Nixon seemed especially miffed, because he no longer was our solo floor leader. He had to go back to sharing the point guard spot with Magic. I was surprised at the resentment. We had been holding the fort long enough without Magic. I now wanted things to be easier, but no such luck.

We only had twelve games left in the regular season to work Magic back into the groove. He was playing hard and not fearful of injury, but his quickness was not there. He was making fakes with the ball and running into people. Defenses were able to stop him. We were to play a crucial game at home against the Phoenix Suns for first place in the Pacific Division. Phoenix had been outstanding all year, and yet here we were right on their heels. This was to be Magic Johnson's real coming-out party, when it counted. We played without Mike Cooper, who was ill, and lost a close game to the Suns. Magic was just fair, and it was obvious he needed more time to get ready. I hoped twelve games would be enough.

During the final week of the season, we seemed to be coming together. We won three games in three nights, and the middle game was a win at Portland, where the Lakers had always struggled. Our team spirit was improving, but our luck was not. Jamaal Wilkes was injured on a drive to the hoop in Portland. His back was very sore, and he acted gun-shy the rest of the year. While Norm Nixon was absent after his grandmother passed away, the team lost at Salt Lake City. During that game, Kareem exploded at the officials and was ejected. On his way to the locker room, he karate kicked the Jazz water cooler into the fifth row.

During our last game of the season against Denver, I decided to rest Jamaal and Kareem and play our reserves along with Magic Johnson to give them one last run before the playoffs. It was a run-and-shoot game, and Magic was dominating the action. Maybe he was back. We had a chance to win it in the closing seconds. I called our No. 41 series, which spread the court and gave Magic the ball to come down the lane to pass or shoot. It was the same play set that won our final game last season at Golden State. Magic dribbled the ball into position and then, with six seconds remaining, made his move. But he was called for a charging foul, and we eventually lost the game to the Nuggets. The good fortune of our championship season was not as generous this year.

But now the new season, the playoffs, was beginning. Last year we had won our division and were rewarded with a first-round bye. This year we were division runners-up to Phoenix and had to get by the miniseries. As the regular season closed, there were three possible teams we could open with in the playoffs: Kansas City, Golden State, or Houston. The only team we feared was the Houston Rockets. They were a hot-and-cold team who, with Moses Malone, were capable of beating anyone on any given night. This was a very dangerous team in a miniseries. With our bad luck, the Houston Rockets won a playoff berth against us on the last day of the season.

We had two days to prepare for the Rockets. I rested the team the first day and went hard the second. Everything was fine. We had survived our injuries and the pressures of being champions. We were an experienced team who knew how to win in the playoffs. I told our team we were ready for another run for the gold rings. But the first sign of trouble occurred during our final shootaround the day of the game. There was an article in the *LA Times* revealing Nixon's displeasure with the return of Magic Johnson. Norm Nixon disliked his new role on the team with Magic now handling the ball. During our final preparation, Magic was sullen and bent out of shape. Obviously, he had read the article and was in a deep funk. I spoke to him and tried to perk him up, but he rolled his eyes in utter frustration. This was supposed to be a moment of coming together and pooling all our energies for the playoffs, but suddenly, we were in disarray.

We opened at home in the Forum against the Rockets and lost. We played decent, but Moses Malone was unstoppable, scoring 39 points and getting twenty-four rebounds. My fear of the hot-and-cold Rockets had materialized; they were hot.

In the locker room, Magic was beside himself with anger. After everyone left, he complained to me about the infighting among the players. All season, Jim Chones had been on Kareem; Nixon was attacking Magic; and as we left the court tonight, Mike Cooper was complaining that Jamaal Wilkes wasn't playing any defense. Magic warned that he was going to clear the air with the team in Houston.

Unfortunately, Magic couldn't wait until we met the next day in Houston. While on the flight down to Texas, Magic talked to Rich Levin of the *Herald Examiner* and unloaded all his frustrations. He concluded by saying the team was jealous of him and all his lucrative *deals*. So instead of putting the team problems to rest, Magic opened up a whole new chapter for the remaining days of the series.

The second game of the miniseries was in Houston and a must win for us, or we would be eliminated. I made every adjustment necessary to counter our previous defeat. We had to make the game go at a quicker pace so that we could get our running game in high gear. Houston was playing walk-it-down-and-milk-the-clock basketball, which was death to us. I decided to start Mike Cooper ahead of Jim Chones to allow us to full-court press on defense and run like the wind on offense. I was going to utilize our speed against Houston's slowdown tactics. I felt confident it would work, but I feared that sitting Jim Chones would cause another upheaval. Because of this, I decided not to tell the team of my switch until game time. I didn't want them grumbling during the day. I was determined to get a win tonight at any price.

During that afternoon, Pat Riley, who was the only one who knew my plans, told our PR guy, Bruce Jolesch, that something was up for tonight's game. There was going to be a shuffling in the starting lineup. With this information, Jolesch went to the CBS-TV pregame strategy meeting and told them Magic Johnson was not going to start and that they had a scoop. How he came up with this, I'll never know.

The rumor of Magic being benched spread to the LA writers, and they confronted Jerry Buss. Not knowing anything about it, he got excited and called Bill Sharman to find out what was going on. No one ever contacted me, because they knew better than to question a game-strategy decision. The real lineup switch was announced as planned just prior to game time, and we went on the floor with our quick greyhounds.

Walking on the court to start the game, I noticed the referee Jake O'Donnell at center court. This is bad news for me and for the Lakers. Even though Jake and I were both from Philadelphia, he had it in for me and our team. Last season, during a game in Phoenix, O'Donnell called a technical foul on Magic Johnson. I stood up with a puzzled expression, and he called a T on me. My guess is that Jake wanted to send a message that no rookie player like Magic or rookie coach like Paul Westhead was going to question his authority. We could come and go; he was a permanent fixture.

Every game since Phoenix, Jake seemed to have an issue with us. I went to our bench in Houston with my head down, not making eye contact with center court. Jake cried out in a loud voice, "Westy, Westy, you are going to be okay tonight. The Rockets hate me more than you do." We were going to need to execute well to beat Houston, but having Jake O'Donnell on our side wouldn't hurt.

We started the game like a flash of lightning. Everything was working to perfection. Our pressing defense and fast break offense had quickened the pace. We were in control of the tempo. Houston closed our lead just prior to halftime, but we were in good shape.

During my halftime talk to the team, Jerry Buss appeared in the back of the room. Very unusual. Buss had never come to our locker room at halftime. He listened to my comments as if his life depended on the outcome. He had a frantic look on his face. I was glad he wasn't making the decisions for the second half. We went out and played a convincing second half. Late in the game, we had a 2-point lead, and Magic got called for his sixth personal foul and left the game. As Magic was being replaced, I stood up and looked at Jake O'Donnell in disbelief. He said to me, "I didn't make the call, dummy."

We made a defensive stop and won the game. After the game, everyone was emotionally tired from our do-or-die win but seemingly happy and together.

The day of the final game, I felt confident we would win. I studied the films of both games and clearly saw we were on the right course with starting Mike Cooper and pushing the fast pace. But as I talked to the team in the locker room about our strategy, they seemed distant. They were looking at me but not paying attention. Something was bothering them in addition to the pressure of a big game. As soon as I completed my most important pregame talk of the season, Magic Johnson called over to Norm Nixon, trying to explain that he didn't mean to ridicule him and other teammates in the newspaper. Instead of reviewing how to handle Calvin Murphy, our players were walking onto the court trying to clarify their loyalty to one another. Their concern over the morning's sports page was an obvious distraction for that afternoon's important activity.

The game was typical of the last in a series, both teams working hard, not shooting the ball or executing offense well because of the tenacious defense. Magic Johnson was trying his best but couldn't make a basket. He was firing bricks all over the court. Mike Cooper, who started for the second straight time, was having an awful game. He couldn't get any rhythm. His free throws didn't even hit the rim. Despite his poor showing, my decision to start him for a faster team was a valid move. Mike Cooper just wasn't ready for this contest. Jamaal Wilkes was scoring well with his classic twenty-foot jump shot that, for Jamaal, was like a lay-up. But his defense was erratic, and he had to sit on the bench due to early foul trouble. Our other two starters, Norm Nixon and Kareem Abdul-Jabbar, were having a normal game. The two of them were converting our most basic play, called "the fist," for easy baskets.

Our fist play had been the center of controversy with the players all season long. This play was signaled by the point guard putting his fist up in the air. It meant the guard was to dribble down Kareem's side and in so doing push the forward on that side away from Kareem. In effect, we were creating a two-man play with only one pass necessary to complete the set. It was as simple as dribbling the ball down below the foul line and delivering the ball to the tallest and best player in the world and letting him take care of the rest. One of my major team principles was to get the ball to Kareem in the low post on a frequent basis. I had strong feelings that there was a direct relationship between delivering the goods to Kareem and winning. Other players, especially our guards, had different ideas. This was a constant battle, and only Kareem's unbelievable consistency and accuracy made them tolerate my demand.

I could remember at the start of this miniseries against Houston saying, "Nixon must get the ball below the foul line extended on the dribble fist play." This instruction was crucial because Norm Nixon, game after game, insisted on picking his dribble up too high above the foul line. When the defense would play in front on Kareem, it was practically impossible to pass in to him from above the foul line. If you dribbled below the foul line, you then exposed the defense, and the entry pass to Kareem was open.

As we went into the final quarter against the Rockets, there were some bright signs that we were going to win. Mark Landsberger had come off the bench and was muscling up to Moses Malone. We finally found someone willing to go toe-to-toe in a street fight with Moses. With Malone in check, the score was tied with less than two minutes to play. Magic Johnson was fouled but missed 2 out of 3 attempts to give us only a 1-point lead. What happened next would decide our entire season.

The Rockets looked to find Moses open around the basket or Calvin Murphy free on the outside. Because of some excellent defense, especially by Cooper on Murphy, the Rockets were forced to scramble. Mike Dunleavy was open because of a communication breakdown involving Kareem and

Nixon. Kareem had momentarily picked up Dunleavy, who was Nixon's man, off a cut to the basket. As soon as Kareem saw that the ball was not going inside to Dunleavy, he released on him and picked up his own man. Nixon lingered inside and failed to see that Dunleavy popped out to help the struggling Calvin Murphy, who couldn't get a shot off the swarming Mike Cooper. Because of a misunderstanding between Nixon and Kareem, neither player went out on Dunleavy, and he received the pass from Murphy and scored the go-ahead basket.

The poetic justice was that there had been continual bad communication between Nixon and Kareem all season. Nixon was the ringleader of suggesting, "We do too much for Kareem," and Kareem knew it. Without any words spoken, it was evident there was no love lost between Nixon and Kareem. Thus, their failure to talk things out in this important moment was an extension of their feelings all along.

During the ensuing time-out, I set up a play to regain the lead and hopefully win the game. It was money time, and I went with the man, Kareem Abdul-Jabbar. The play was one we had run hundreds of times before at end-of-quarter and end-of-game situations. It was a 1-4 set with a double stack on the low post. From that stack, we would pop the players out wide, leaving Kareem alone in the low-post area. It was the primary objective of the point guard—in this case, Magic Johnson—to deliver the ball to Kareem in the low post. This was the play; this was what we explicitly said to do in the time-out. Any alternative actions were to come *only* if Kareem was not open and available. I made the decision to have Magic handle and not Nixon because Magic was better at improvising when the basic plan was taken away by smart defense. And also it put Nixon and Wilkes out wide for the perimeter shot if necessary. In this crucial play, our fifth player was Mike Cooper, who initially played the opposite post and then popped up the lane to be in a position to pass the ball to Kareem.

We decided to take the ball underneath and go the full length of the court for the last shot rather than exercise our option to get it at half court. There would be less congestion and threat of interception from the baseline, and since there were fourteen seconds remaining, we had plenty of time. The ball was inbounded to Magic, and he very deliberately brought it up court as the other four players went deep into the shell of our low-post stack.

With eight seconds remaining, Magic reached the top of the key area, which triggered the other players to fan out to their spots. To my utter surprise, the Rockets pursued our players stride for stride as they ran to their spread positions. My guess going into the play was that Houston would sag in and make it difficult for us to pass inside to Kareem. But no, here they were in a spread-out, matchup defense. This meant the entry pass in to Kareem was to be much simpler than anticipated.

Magic, however, did not read the situation. He did not look for his primary target, Kareem, who was open in the low post. Houston's defense gave Magic an open passing angle to Kareem. He scratched the first option and decided to go one-on-one himself. Instead of this being Magic's final choice, he made it his first move. He shot a running jumper above the free-throw line and missed. The fact that it turned out to be an air ball and we lost the game was not Magic's biggest mistake. To miss is human, and I would defend him for that. The greater breach was his attempt to win the game by taking it into his own hands and not giving it up to Kareem. Magic wanted the season to rest on his shoulders, even if placing it on Kareem's was a better idea.

Magic Johnson decided to take the role of the star in his hands. He knew this was the crucial moment reserved for the star to deliver the goods. He showed the guts of a budding star who dared to try and win for his team. Magic, like Kareem, felt he had earned the star position, and with that role went the right to take the final shot. In this instance, Magic unfortunately chose the wrong star.

13

Twenty-Five Million Reasons

After the game, everyone was like a zombie, unable to believe it was over. There was nothing to say, other than preserving the dignity and style of a champion. There was no use for harsh words or criticism at this time. It was obvious that Magic felt embarrassed; we lost with him taking the last shot. It wasn't his fault we lost. You don't lose a game on one shot. Magic, however, was unaccustomed to this feeling of failure and the strong overtones that he was a heavy in the outcome.

A couple of weeks later, during a CBS interview with Brent Musburger, Magic seemed to be blaming others for the failure of the Lakers and not willing to take his fair share of our shortcomings. He stated that some trades were necessary for us to return to our championship form. The burden of being the man, after a season-ending play, was not sitting well with Magic Johnson.

A couple of days after his CBS interview, I saw Magic at the Forum, and he came to me and wanted to talk for a few moments. He seemed beside himself and blurted out, "You know what I meant to say about the team. I didn't mean to blame others or demand they be traded." I calmed him down and reassured him that I knew his intentions were good and that he tried his best to win the game. For the first time since I had known Magic, he seemed to be carrying around a bundle of guilt for what went wrong, and he didn't like the burden.

Jerry Buss saw me after the game and wanted to talk. Somehow, I was the only one who could appreciate the depth of his disappointment. He rambled about the outcome like a parent receiving notice that his child was missing in action. We agreed to meet in a few days and went our separate ways.

The following day, we had our final team meeting. I was brief with my comments but stressed to the players the importance of accepting the defeat gracefully. I instructed them to avoid blaming one another for our demise and to carry themselves like world champions. I stressed the future to them and the importance of coming back next season determined to recapture our crown.

My evaluation of the season was that we didn't have enough time to blend Magic Johnson back into working with the rest of the team. We almost made it, but with Moses Malone and the miniseries, we ran out of time.

I knew that if it happened again, my time as Lakers head coach would have run out.

I was convinced that the major adjustment necessary to regain our championship form was to acquire a legitimate power forward. We needed a tough, physical player who would complement the finesse style of Jamaal Wilkes and Kareem Abdul-Jabbar. In my opinion, we could win another world championship if we could unload Jim Chones and pick up Mitch Kupchak.

We had tried to work a deal with the Washington Bullets during the regular season for Kupchak. But at that time, the Bullets wanted Norm Nixon, and our front office wasn't serious enough to make a deal. But a few weeks after the trade deadline, I received a note from Jerry Buss telling me of Dean Smith's recommendation of his former player, Mitch Kupchak. Once Jerry Buss heard coach Smith's high praise, he thought Kupchak would be a terrific player for us. I thought it funny that he was paying me a big salary to coach his team, yet he would listen more to free advice from the outside. In this instance, it corroborated my position, so I was happy.

Jerry Buss also met individually with some of our key players after the season, and they unanimously felt that we needed a power forward and that he should be none other than Mitch Kupchak. Now with this confirmation of my evaluation, Jerry Buss informed me that he was ready to "go to the vault" for Kupchak.

In July 1981 Mitch Kupchak finally signed an offer sheet with the Lakers. I was jubilant over the deal but knew the Bullets would have fifteen days to match the offer or trade him off to another team. It was like being invited to a banquet and seeing all the sumptuous food but unable to enter until the doors were unlocked. The Bullets claimed that they would sign Kupchak and not unlock the door for our feast. They would do anything to avoid giving him to us for nothing. There were rumors that the Bullets were working on a trade with the Knicks for Marvin Webster and another deal with the Philadelphia 76ers for Darryl Dawkins. There was the possibility that they may agree to lesser quality players just to get something rather than give Kupchak away to us.

But we got some information that Washington didn't have any substantial deal in the process, so it looked like we would get Mitch Kupchak. I then attempted to kill two birds with one stone by suggesting we offer some future draft picks along with Jim Chones. Since we seemed to have the upper hand, I proposed giving them some of what they wanted and coupling it with what we and they didn't want—namely, Chones. The Bullets agreed to take a couple of draft choices with Brad Holland and Chones to solidify our acquisition of Kupchak. We agreed, and the final piece of our future success was complete. I knew people were going to think that we got hustled by the Bullets, but the Kupchak-Chones swap just cleared the way for an NBA championship.

The irony of this achievement was that it turned out to be a major factor in my being fired. Jerry Buss always felt as if I had forced his hand in the Kupchak deal. Whenever Mitch Kupchak looked bad in a game, Jerry Buss would transfer his frustration over to me as the engineer of the deal. Whenever the press commented that we needed a backup center, Buss was angered that I forced him to give up Jim Chones. There were also some players who felt as though I railroaded Chones out of town. I was not fazed by any of this, because I was confident the deal was going to bring us the championship. That was worth all the abuse.

AS THE DAYS of the summer rolled on, the blundered last shot of Magic Johnson seemed to fade into oblivion. With the announcement of Magic's new contract of $25 million for twenty-five years, however, comments about Magic's position on the team were brought up again. Kareem demanded to be traded to the New York Knicks if Magic had indeed been crowned leader for life by Jerry Buss.

Consequently, a meeting was set up with Kareem and Buss, during which time I was asked by Buss to be available. Jerry Buss, like our players, recognized that the relationship between Kareem and I was strong and that he would listen to me and respect my feelings on this and other team matters. I was never called on to be a part of that meeting. Later that same afternoon, a press conference was called, and Jerry Buss delivered an explanation of Magic Johnson's new contract, the richest in sports at the time.

He clarified to the press that Magic was not to be considered a part of management even though his contract was for many years after his playing days were over. He publicly apologized to Kareem for this misunderstanding and said the problem was in Buss's failure to properly explain the exact nature of Magic's contract. What was coming across loud and clear was that Jerry Buss was backing down in public for Kareem's sake, but the cause of this embarrassment was Magic, for whom Buss had the highest personal regard. The battle lines between Magic and Kareem were becoming stronger. This last incident clearly entrenched Buss and Magic on one side and Kareem on the other.

Magic had been struggling to take symbolic charge of the team ever since we won the world championship. After Magic started at center for the injured Kareem in that final game, he felt that it was his team and his position as leader. During the next season, as early as training camp, Magic was flexing his muscles as team leader over Kareem.

In light of Magic's attempt to take charge of the team, he became increasingly uncomfortable with my emphasis on a game plan highlighting Kareem. I honestly feel that the final blow against me at my firing was a blow against Kareem. Not the person Kareem but the player. The man who drew all the attention. The man who got the most interest from his coach. The man who dictated the pace of the game. And most importantly, the man to whom we always gave the ball at the end of the game.

Magic wanted to be that man. He wanted that position of importance and respect. I had, from the start, made the decision that Kareem was the man to go to for all crucial plays, and Magic was going to tear away at that position. I saw all the conflict around me building up but failed to see that I would be lined up on the side of Kareem and not on the side of the entire team.

14

Lakers Doth Protest Too Much

I was excited about the opening of training camp in Palm Springs for the 1981–82 season. I believed we had the personnel to win big this season, and it was now time to blend our talents together into a smooth unit.

I decided to install my fast break system and put aside the offense that got us an NBA championship. Logic would say to keep the same offense that won for you, that got you a new contract and a new championship ring.

But something inside me said change—do your thing. Do what you believe is the best offensive scheme in basketball. Coach the way you want the game to go. I believed in the fast break. I believed it would make us better. I wanted to do something to avoid losing early in the playoffs and to win another championship. With the acquisition of Mitch Kupchak and the repair of Magic Johnson's knee, I felt that we had the personnel to run the break. Now I had to teach the system and drill the players until it was second nature, and then we would show the world that the Lakers were on top once again.

To my surprise, my new offense did not go over well with the players. They resisted the demand for maximum speed on every offensive possession. NBA players like to pick and choose when to go fast and when to slow down and walk it up on offense. They want a steady, controlled pace. My system demanded speed to the max on every offensive possession.

After our first practice, eyes were rolling in disbelief; I could see the players asking themselves, "Is this how we're going to practice and play the whole season?" The final drill on day one was to run the lines—or as it is also known in college circles, "murders."

As a group, the players sprinted the full court ten times down and back. Walking off the court toward the locker room, Kareem came over to me and said, "Paul, I don't do murders," and walked away. He did this for one day but was clearly saying it would not happen again.

I was appreciative of his one and only gesture and smart enough to never run murders again.

Incidentally, Kareem never addressed me as "Coach." I was always "Paul," like a peer in the Lakers family. Kareem only called one man coach—John Wooden.

My opening address to the team stressed an end to players blaming one another for the team losing a game. I even inserted a fine of up to $500 for players who made public comments about a teammate's performance. Ironically, they stopped the bickering among themselves, like the Magic Johnson and Norm Nixon newspaper feud, and turned their displeasure on someone they had in common—me.

The opening practice sessions demonstrated the willingness of our players to work hard and recapture our lost title. It was the best training camp we'd had in three years. Kareem Abdul-Jabbar was in good condition and was leading the way as team captain. Because of the all-out effort, there were many scrapes and bruises in this camp, and many of the collisions centered on Mitch Kupchak. He was a delight to watch with his unlimited hustle, and his hardworking attitude was contagious. There were no cheap fist fights on the court this training camp, although the inner struggle between Kareem and Jerry Buss was still very much alive off the court.

One evening during training camp in Palm Springs, we had just finished our workout at the College of the Desert, and I was sitting off to the side with Jerry Buss, who had come down to see the team practice. As we talked, different players would stroll by to say hello. Some rookies would come over and hope to befriend Buss so that they could stay on longer than just training camp. As we talked, Kareem came walking by, and Jerry Buss yelled a big hello out to Kareem. He looked over at us, turned his head, and walked by without a comment or gesture of greeting. It was a clear sign to Buss: Kareem obviously couldn't care less.

At that moment, I felt sorry for Buss, who had paid Kareem so much money and who had made a public apology to sooth Kareem and now could not even get a cordial greeting from his leading actor. The deeper frustration for Buss was that he could not do very much about it. Later that week, Jerry invited everyone to dinner at a Japanese steak house. Everyone was there in respectful attendance except one, Kareem Abdul-Jabbar. Kareem was above him and untouchable. Jerry Buss could only retaliate against those who were associated with Kareem, like his coach.

Buss told me on different occasions about his contractual dealings with Kareem and how he had gotten the upper hand on him. During my first year with the Lakers, Buss talked about how all Kareem's new money was an easy give away for him. Some of it was bonus money based solely on winning the NBA title. Other parts were based on giving Kareem the use of the Forum for a few nights a year free of charge to put on shows and other events. Buss related how insignificant that was, since the nights would be dark anyway (with no other engagements scheduled) and he would make it up on the concessions. Consequently, he was going to make money on what appeared to be a most generous gift to his superstar.

Just prior to the summer summit conference between Buss and Kareem, I met with Jerry, who told me he thought we were in deep trouble with Kareem. He felt as if Kareem really might demand to be traded to the Knicks. He felt the strongest dislike for Kareem's agent, Tom Collins, and with Collins and Kareem together, Buss feared that he may not be able to smooth things out. Buss was pinning all the blame on Collins, saying he was the one who was whispering into Kareem's ear to demand a trade.

The summit meeting resolved most of the surface issues—namely, that Magic Johnson, for the time being, was not to be considered as management. Magic was simply a player like Kareem, and therefore, on the surface, Kareem was still *the man*. But unresolved were all the bad feelings voiced between Jerry Buss and Tom Collins. Jerry Buss had not won this negotiation with Kareem and wasn't happy about it.

My last meeting with Jerry Buss before we went to training camp was again in his private office at the Forum. By that time, the Mitch Kupchak deal had been finalized, and we reviewed the reaction around the league. Buss admitted that he received a great deal of heat over Kupchak from fellow owners. Some felt as though he was foolish for spending millions of dollars on a substitute with a bad back; others felt as though he was buying himself another potential championship by using astronomical amounts of cash. Many owners feared the ripple effect of matching salaries like Kupchak's for their players, which for some would mean bankruptcy.

Buss forewarned me that teams throughout the league would be after us to hopefully expose the folly of our deal. It was going to be "Get this one against the Lakers for the owner." I appreciated Buss's frankness about his personal concern, but I already saw that the one on the firing line was me, not him. If we faltered and had a poor season, heads were going to roll, and mine happened to be one of the least expensive.

Clearly, the simplest adjustment would be to get a new coach. Not in my wildest dreams, however, did I see the possibility of getting fired during the regular season. I felt as though I had earned the right to play this poker hand till the last card was dealt. It was unthinkable that I could be fired with my track record with this team. I had the best winning percentage of any active NBA coach and the best playoff percentage record. I was sure I held enough cards to play out the season.

THE PRESEASON NBA Board of Governors meeting where Jerry Buss was exposed by his fellow owners as hurting the league had clearly bothered Buss. He told me Harry Mangurian, owner of the Boston Celtics, stood up and lashed out at Buss for his contract dealings with players over the summer. Buss told me he was so hurt that he went immediately to his hotel room and avoided the traditional cocktails and camaraderie after the meetings. I believe this incident left a deep wound inside Buss and that he was determined to show his peers that he was right. By winning another world championship—and in so doing, taking the crown away from the Boston Celtics—Buss could come out a genius. If the Lakers lost, it would be Jerry Buss, the buffoon. Jerry Buss was so frightened of being labeled a fool that he wanted the Lakers not only to win most of their games but to do it with blazing excitement.

I know this because during the summer, while vacationing with my family in Hawaii, I received a call from Buss. This was unusual to begin with. Such a call was reserved for urgent matters, and for Buss this was such an occasion. He told me the owners had berated him over the Kupchak deal and that he demanded that we not only win but "win big" this upcoming season. His message was clear. It was not enough to win games; we had to do it convincingly.

We entered the final week of practice before our season opener in good shape. The new part of our offense was rough around the edges, but that was understandable, and the players were cooperating with the system. We ran into a snag when Kareem reported out sick for a couple of days. We just couldn't advance our preparation with him absent. As in the past, Norm Nixon complained about Kareem calling in sick and quizzed our trainer about the illness. Nixon wanted to know if Kareem went to the doctor and if he was going to be fined for missing practice without permission.

We opened the season at home against the very team that eliminated us in the miniseries last season, the Houston Rockets. We had been waiting six months for a chance to get back at the Rockets and now we are ready. We got off to a slow start, with Magic missing a couple of open lay-ups. Obviously, the team felt the pressure to win big and settle the account with the Rockets. Except for Norm Nixon, who was razor sharp, the starters were sluggish. Jamaal Wilkes was having an off night shooting. Kareem was slow moving up and down the court. His reactions were sluggish due to his recent bout with the flu. Mitch Kupchak was so jittery that he couldn't even catch the ball.

We finally caught the Rockets late in the game and sent it into overtime. In the closing seconds of overtime, we went ahead by 1 and now had to hold Houston scoreless on their last attempt. They came down court, and Tom Henderson missed a driving hook shot. Magic Johnson rebounded the ball with eleven seconds left and dribbled up court, seemingly to seal our victory. During a time-out, we had just discussed that if the Rockets scored and went ahead by 1 point, we would call an immediate time-out, but if we got possession on their miss, we would dribble it up and go into our five-up spread offense and kill the clock. For some reason, Magic was confused and looked over to the bench. I frantically signaled him to run our five-up play. He in turn took a couple of more dribbles and called a time-out. All he needed to do was dribble it out, and we would have won. Now we had to inbound the ball and run the clock out again.

As fate would have it, the inbound pass from Jamaal to Kareem was deflected out of bounds, and Houston got possession. We now had to stop Houston one more time to win. In the final second, the ball went inside to Moses Malone, who stumbled as he was swarmed by three defenders. He nonetheless staggered to the hoop and flipped in the winning basket.

It was a brutal defeat after waiting six months to get back in action. All the bad feelings of losing the miniseries that took months to forget were now vividly in our face. We couldn't have suffered a worse defeat if it had been planned by our bitterest enemy.

I decided to take the following day off to soothe our wounds, but at practice the day after that, the players were still stunned by the Houston loss. Normally, they were very good at pushing aside a tough loss, because they had eighty-one other games to deal with and they had to be ready each night.

Sensing their struggle to bounce back, I talked to them about hanging together and growing stronger as we absorb our mutual problems. This attempt to share the problem and build together for the future seemed to help everyone except Magic Johnson. He wanted no part of the team's energy. All during practice, Magic remained distant from everyone. Once again, Magic was having trouble handling defeat, especially when he was a part of the final breakdown.

No one blamed Magic for the loss with his inappropriate time-out, yet he was acting as if everyone else was wrong except him. Magic liked to pass the problem off to others. In his mind we should never have turned the ball over on our last out of bounds, or we needed to run a different offense. But the difficulty was not going to rest with him. It was too close to the embarrassment he experienced in our miniseries finale last season, and Magic Johnson was determined not to be the fall guy this time around. Consequently, he stayed in a funky mood for days, long after others were getting back into their normal rhythm.

After our nightmare with Houston, we went on the road to Portland and Seattle. This was just what we didn't need at this time. Portland was always tough against us on their home court—particularly, early in the season. Their coach, Jack Ramsay, did an exceptionally fine job of getting his team ready for the opening of the season. In this regard, the first dozen games in the NBA should not be used as a barometer of a team's strength and eventual position in the league. What frequently happens is the better teams with solid veterans start out slow and work themselves into a playing groove. On the other hand, the weaker teams with younger, insecure players are going full throttle from day one. They must look good early to attract the fans, because they know things will catch up with them in the end. Portland was a combination of a good solid team that was ready at the opening game.

As we prepared for Portland, I couldn't believe how our team seemed devastated over one loss. During our shootaround, they were clowning around and not in a work mood. They were feeling the pressure to win and were acting flip and casual. Our performance that night was like a roller coaster. We went up 10 points in the early going and went down 18 points by halftime. We played well in the last quarter but lost at the buzzer on a clutch basket by Kelvin Ransey deep from the corner.

We were now 0-2, and the writers were already asking what was wrong with the team. We lost two games by a whisker, and already the buzzards were circling. At this juncture, I felt that a great injustice was at work— people assuming there were critical problems after two early season losses. There was more evidence showing that we were a compatible group who would settle down and win big. Sure, we were using a new offense for a significant portion of the game, and it was still strange to them. But that wasn't unusual early in the season. My emphasis on a new set offense was to improve our transition from the running game to our slow-down half-court offense. Last season, in the playoffs, Houston slowed the pace of the game down and forced us into a more deliberate half-court offense, so my new emphasis this season was to improve our half-court offense so that there would be no repeat of that.

What I suspect happened was when the players were asked by the press about our slow start, the convenient thing to point to was the new offense.

The truth was, at this stage of an eighty-two-game season, it was no one's fault. We simply were unlucky in the first two games. With the media pushing the panic button, it compounded the damage. As a result, we went to Seattle for game three with our players acting as if they were on a thirty-game losing streak.

At the start of the Seattle game, we were awful. We were making fundamental errors that never happened in any of our training work. We were sluggish getting back on defense, and Gus Williams destroyed us on the break. In no time, we were down 18 points and sinking fast. At halftime I tried to regroup our squad by reminding them that we had been down like this before against Seattle and had come back to win. In fact, we had a twelve-game winning streak over the Sonics.

In the second half, we made a great comeback and won in the last minute; more importantly, we had won our first game of the season. What a sense of relief it was to get into the win column, especially when it looked as if we were about to lose our third straight.

We returned home for a game with the Phoenix Suns, the team that had beaten us out for the Pacific Division title the previous year and forced us into the miniseries. We were determined to turn that around this season and get a bye in the first round of the playoffs.

Suddenly, there were signs of improvement. Mitch Kupchak, after an awful opening game, was now playing very well. He was complementing Kareem on the boards exactly as we planned.

But Magic Johnson was still struggling. He was unwilling to cooperate with the program unless it was on his terms. During the game, Magic ran at his pace. When he felt like pushing the ball on the fast break, he went hard, when he didn't, he strolled. He also picked and chose when he would work at executing our set offense. Sometimes, Magic would set a good screen, and other times, he would go through the motions. As I saw it, Magic's major problem was that he was struggling to get by defenders who were easy marks before his knee injury, and now, out of frustration, he was finding fault with the system.

For the most part, we were not sharp against Phoenix, but in the last quarter, we closed their 10-point lead and tied the game with a three-point shot by Magic. There were twenty seconds remaining, giving the Suns a last shot opportunity. They isolated Kyle Macy with the ball at the top of the key, and he worked on Norm Nixon and finally made a tough eighteen-footer to win the game.

After the loss, the press was critical of me for putting Nixon on Macy. To me that didn't make sense; Norm Nixon was a tough competitor who was not giving up a size advantage to Macy. If Nixon couldn't handle Kyle Macy in a clutch situation, then he shouldn't be our starting guard. When it's crunch time, you can't play hide-and-seek with your key players. Otherwise, you need to get new key players.

After the game, Jerry Buss requested to meet with me and Bill Sharman. My guess was that he wanted to ask how we could get the team on a winning streak. To my surprise, it was not about the game but about a potential trade for Norm Nixon. The Phoenix Suns asked Buss if he would be interested in Dennis Johnson for Norm Nixon.

Jerry Buss seemed excited about it and asked what we thought. Bill Sharman was all for it. He pointed out tonight's game as an example of Nixon's poor defense costing us games. Like the David Thompson trade possibility last year, everything was a go for trading Nixon except for my approval. Once again, I said no. We needed Nixon. I knew he hated my guts, but I also knew he came to play. If the same situation with Macy and Nixon happened again, I would be very confident in going with Nixon.

Coincidentally, the same circumstance took place one week later in Phoenix. In this instance, Macy missed and we won. After the victory, our press said my decision to put Nixon on Macy was either stubborn or lucky.

After our Forum loss to Phoenix, we were 1-3, and everyone was looking around to blame someone else for the problem. Magic was implying that it was our offense; so did the media. One paper reported that Jerry Buss had given me a vote of confidence. It said Buss realized it was very early in the season and that you cannot evaluate a team until they play around twenty games. I was upset with the vote-of-confidence line. It was like coming home late for dinner a few nights and your wife announcing to the neighborhood that she still loves you.

We got a break in the schedule by playing Dallas at home and won, though it was not a smooth performance. Our players were still not in the groove and needed more wins to mesh. Some of the things we always did well, such as the outside shooting of Jamaal Wilkes, were not happening. Jamaal was off to a horrible start. He couldn't make an open fifteen-foot jumper, which normally was like a lay-up for him. I was not overly concerned about Jamaal, because he was such a consistent player. I knew this was a fleeting problem for him.

We went on our second road trip of the season with games at San Antonio and Houston. We had a team meeting about being more productive. I made some adjustments to clear up some snags in the offense. We went through the changes on the floor and had a crisp, alert practice session. This carried over into the game, and we started out very sharp. Our fast break and set offense were more fluid. Then in about the middle of the second quarter, we ran out of gas, and San Antonio steamrollered over us.

From that moment to the end of the game, we played the worst basketball I'd seen since I had been with the Lakers. San Antonio destroyed us, and we gave up without a fight. Jamaal Wilkes had another awful-shooting night. The only player who went hard the entire game was Magic Johnson. After the game, Magic was grumbling out of frustration, and rightfully so, because most of his teammates gave up long before the buzzer. Magic implied to the press that the fault lay with the coach and his offense. He was careful not to blame any of his teammates as he had after the Houston miniseries, so he unloaded his anger at losing on the next visible object—me.

I get it, but it totally ignored the real reason we lost. We allowed twenty-eight uncontested fast breaks and slam dunks in our face. No offense is able to absorb that many giveaways.

The following day on our trip to Houston, Kareem called me aside to have a private discussion. Those traveling with us had to assume that it was about the San Antonio game and our 2-4 record. It was, however, about the personal plight of Jamaal Wilkes. He had gone to Kareem during the night and expressed his desire to leave the team for an extended period. He had experienced a tragedy with the death of his infant daughter just before training camp and now felt unable to concentrate on the game. He wanted some time off to clear his mind. He knew his ineffective play was hurting the team and felt he should leave for a while. Kareem advised Jamaal to complete the trip and then go home and decide his fate.

Later, I spoke to Jamaal about his problem and encouraged him that whatever he decided, we would support him. If he took off, I would understand, or if he stayed, I would absorb his ineffective play until he cleared his mind. Jamaal was very appreciative and began to show signs of improvement. Those outside Kareem and me were blaming my new offense for Jamaal's ineffective shooting. I found it humorous how people will find the solutions to things that fit what they want them to be, not necessarily what the truth is.

When we arrived in Houston, Magic sat alone on the sidewalk, waiting for the luggage to be loaded onto our bus. I assume Magic's isolation was an outward sign of his blaming the team for our poor play. Ironically, the spirit of the team was better, and we played that way. Jamaal Wilkes hit some outside shots. We caught the Rockets at the end and had a chance to win on a final out-of-bounds play. We had already lost two games by not executing well at the end. But this time we called a special play for Nixon, and it worked. He made a jump shot to win the game. For the first time this season, there was real happiness in the locker room. We were returning home with a 3-4 record but with the tide turned in our direction.

Despite a hard-earned win, there was still a heavy atmosphere around the team. Everywhere we went, all eyes were on us as if we were about to explode. At home I got a call from our scout Mike Thibault, who warned me that he didn't like what he was hearing around our front office. He informed me that Jerry West was talking unfavorably about me and the team. The following day, Jerry West came to me and told me he was concerned about the team and that if I wanted anything from him, he would be willing to help. He emphatically stressed that he didn't want to coach the Lakers. I was puzzled by his emphasis on not wanting to coach. At the moment, it reminded me of Hamlet's view of his mother at the mock play depicting the death of his father: "The lady doth protest too much."

In retrospect, the only person who came forward and told me to watch out for my job was my roadman Mike Thibault. Either no one else knew, or they chose not to inform me.

15

No One's Getting Fired

We are such stuff as dreams are made on.

—WILLIAM SHAKESPEARE, *The Tempest*

Our next challenge was unique in professional sports—namely, three games in three nights at different sites. We had to play Portland at home, travel to Phoenix, and return home the third day to meet the Indiana Pacers. This weekend would tell a great deal about the makeup of the Lakers.

During the pregame warm-ups, I met at courtside with Jack Ramsay, the Portland coach, who immediately voiced his concern about the negative comments he was hearing about me. He warned me about how quickly people can turn on you but cautioned me not to get down and be affected by negative publicity. I assured him that I was above the problem and would keep my coaching decisions on target. As we parted to start the game, I saw sincere concern for me in his eyes. His look told me that his friend was in trouble.

We played a sharp game and won convincingly. I used the second team for most of the last quarter and coasted home. Portland was the same team who had beaten us last week, and now we whipped them with ease. We were now on a two-game winning streak, and things had begun to turn for the better. The media, however, seemed disappointed. It was more fun for them when the squeeze was on. Now it was not as exciting; it was too normal to win a couple of games.

Our winning streak would be quickly challenged in Phoenix. We always came up short on their court. I met with the Phoenix press, and they couldn't understand the criticism of the Lakers team and me. Knowing our track record of the past few years, they felt that we were a great team who got off to a slow start and was now getting into the groove.

From the opening tap, we were in high gear against the Suns. Jamaal Wilkes was shooting much better. Our fast break was going well, and we went up by 18 points in the first half. The Suns closed the gap in the second half, and it looked like we were in for the same old story, another loss in Phoenix. We went into the final few minutes and called on Kareem to score inside for us. Unfortunately, he couldn't buy a basket. Kareem got the ball where he wanted it and missed a few easy lay-ups. We couldn't have asked for more, but the big fellow simply missed. On defense, however, we toughened up and shut down the Phoenix rush. A final big defensive play by Mike Cooper on Dennis Johnson saved the game, and we won by a point. This should have been the game to get us over the hump. We had broken the jinx in Phoenix and put together a three-game winning streak.

We had an early morning flight back to Los Angeles to play Indiana. I was beginning to feel more relaxed about the team, until Pat Riley objected to how often we went inside to Kareem. I sensed that he was hearing this old complaint from our players, especially Magic and Norm Nixon. I couldn't believe players were upset with the emphasis on Kareem as the key to winning, in light of his past performance and our victory in Phoenix.

The Indiana game carried a special significance because of Jack McKinney. Jack had been hired by the Pacers in 1980 and had won NBA Coach of the Year honors after leading Indiana to the playoffs for the first time since the ABA-NBA merger. It was obvious how much he would like to beat the Lakers as payback for his mistreatment by the Lakers organization. I felt as though many of the local malcontents would like to see McKinney's team win to emphasize their case against me. I needed to win in order to hold the wolves at bay.

It turned out to be a wild, emotionally filled game, with the Lakers finally winning in double overtime. We had just hit a triple—three wins in three nights. More importantly, we had extended our winning streak to four games. Things should have now settled down to normal. I find it hard to believe, as it was later reported, that Jerry Buss and his advisors made their final decision to fire me after that game. It seems incongruous to fire someone who has just delivered a triple win over the weekend.

We took our winning streak to Salt Lake City and faced the Utah Jazz, who always played particularly hard against us. At the Jazz shootaround, I delivered what was to be my last talk to the Lakers. I first complimented the team for their outstanding effort over the weekend in winning back-to-back-to-back games. I used this achievement as evidence of what hard work will do for a talented team. I stressed that it was not what offensive pattern or defensive matchup they used; it was their talents working to help one another that was the key to winning.

Now that we had established some wins, I wanted the players to reach out for a higher level of performance. Our fast break would improve when players streaked down the court to open the lane for a teammate and not just to get themselves an easy basket. Against Indiana, we had gotten an open jump shot for Jamaal Wilkes because Norm Nixon, Magic Johnson, and Mitch Kupchak ran down ahead of him and gave themselves up to the defense. This unselfishness for others would also pay off in offensive rebounding when they crashed the boards to retrieve a missed shot by a fellow player. One player's effort can cover up for another's misfortune. Once this level of play was reached, our team, with its talent, would be unstoppable.

Our game against the Jazz turned out to be a typical encounter at the Salt Palace. We got the lead but couldn't put them away. Our starters only played hard enough to keep in front. I took a time-out early to remind them that we needed to run the fast break to keep a quick pace. If we went slow, we would be improving Utah's chance to take us to the wire and upset us. Early in the fourth quarter, we opened up a 10-point lead, only to have it trimmed by two straight baskets by Darrell Griffith. I took a time-out to diagram the play Griffith was finding open against us. He was Magic Johnson's man and was getting free on a screen set by Mitch Kupchak's man,

Ben Poquette. During my instruction on how to avoid this play occurring for the third straight time, Magic turned away from the rest of our team.

Magic didn't want to hear anything. I had to chide him to turn and see what we were planning. I reminded him that the game was on the line and that we needed a clear strategy. His response without turning around was, "I'm listening." As in the past, Magic was very sensitive about a problem involving him on the floor. It was always either my fault as coach or some other player's mistake. In this case, Magic was clearly upset with Mitch Kupchak and his failure to help on the screen. The greater goal was to cooperate with one another and win the game. Magic wanted to do it his way and also win the game. I was not willing to take this risk.

In the closing moments of the game, during a time-out, Magic was once again not involved in the huddle. He had turned around, jiving with some fans. Again, I reprimanded him for this and continued with my instruction. He got off the bench in a huff and went out for the final seconds, totally unaware of my plan. As it turned out, we were fortunate to win the game by 3 points—fortunate because Magic had absolutely no idea of our defensive strategy on Utah's final possession.

As we went into the locker room, I decided to clear up my displeasure with Magic's attitude during the time-outs. I felt as if he had gone beyond the limits of a productive player-coach relationship. For the good of the team, I had to stop him now. In an attempt to avoid any unnecessary embarrassment for Magic, I decided not to berate his actions in front of the team but rather to call him aside and tell him face-to-face of my displeasure.

After our postgame team meeting, I beckoned Magic into an empty locker room across the hallway. I then informed him that I would not tolerate his lack of concentration at such a key moment in the game. I was not going to allow Magic to pick and choose when he wanted to cooperate with my team directions. To exercise an option on a play set was one thing, but to sulk and not listen to team strategy at a time-out was unacceptable. I informed him that there would be no more of that ever again. Magic listened and made no response as he returned to the main dressing room.

A sportswriter noticed Magic and me leaving the side room and asked me the nature of our postgame meeting. I responded by saying it was a personal matter and not for public review. When the same question was asked of Magic Johnson, however, he responded with his demand to be traded from the Lakers.

Magic was so accustomed to success and everything going his way that he could not accept valid criticism. I felt that his threats to be traded must be firmly dealt with by me and the Lakers organization. Without holding Magic up to public ridicule, he would, nonetheless, have to stand before the team and accept my direction like all other team members or not play at all. It was clear to me that swift retaliation to Magic's threat would establish his proper place on this team. I didn't seek this dilemma, but I was fully prepared to use it to set the record straight with Magic Johnson.

On the flight back to Los Angeles, I read that there was to be a meeting to resolve the issue. I went directly to my office in the Forum to fill Bill Sharman in with the details of the incident and prepare a strategy for handling Magic. No one was there; nor was there any message of a pending meeting. The media continued to report a meeting of Jerry Buss, Bill Sharman, and myself concerning Magic, but I couldn't get any details.

I kept a previous luncheon engagement with my daughter, Monica, who had been away at college. During lunch, she told me what she thought was going to happen: the Lakers were going to fire me. I laughed at her conclusion and said it sure would be the easiest thing to do, but clearly not the most prudent. I had coached this team to two playoff appearances and one world championship. Did we have issues that season? Of course, every team does, especially that early in the season, but we were handling them, witnessed by our current five-game winning streak. I told her not to worry. We'd get this handled; no one was getting fired.

During our lunch, my office called and told me a meeting with Jerry Buss had been set for 3:00 p.m. My meeting with Buss turned out not to be a discussion of what to do with Magic Johnson. The moment I sat down in his office, he matter-of-factly informed me that I was fired.

I was prepared to work out a resolution in which Magic was told by our organization that he did not dictate policy on trades. I felt as though it was an important time for Jerry Buss to show Magic that he must conform to the team and that no amount of pressure by him would allow Magic to have his own way. In correcting Magic after the Utah Jazz game, I had already made the decision not to permit him to break down team unity on the court. I felt that this was a perfect opportunity for Jerry Buss to show Magic that the owner was in charge of the team off the court. A strong stand now would establish a firm base for future player-management decisions. Unfortunately, Jerry Buss decided not to deal with the Magic Johnson case but, rather, eliminated the problem by firing the coach.

As Jerry Buss explained his decision to fire me, I felt as though he was not being rational in examining the facts. Namely, it was very early in the season, and the team was simply getting its act together for a long eighty-two-game journey before the playoffs. To fire your coach, who had already won a world championship for you less than eighteen months ago, on the sampling of a few games was not a sign of prudence in action. I felt that he had overreacted to the pressure and was under the grip of panic. There was clear evidence of the team shaking its early misfortune, with our current five-game winning streak.

But common sense was not the order of the day after the explosion by Magic Johnson the night before in Salt Lake City. In explaining his decision to dismiss me, Jerry Buss stressed my attempt to slow down the team and deprive them of their freedom to run the fast break. I knew then that temporary insanity had set in, because no one taught, stressed, practiced, or emphasized fast break basketball more than I did. To fire me was one thing, but to do it for the wrong reason, based on bad information, was another thing. I made no attempt to plea bargain for my job, but I did attempt to clarify that from the beginning to my last game against the Jazz, I stressed the running game. At least I wanted the satisfaction of being fired for an accurate reason.

Jerry Buss said, even though the team was winning, they were not exciting enough. He wanted showtime, and mere victories were not sufficient. He cited Jamaal Wilkes as an example of a thrilling offensive player who was off to a terrible start because of my slow-down offense. He was not aware of Jamaal's personal problem and how it hampered his performance. Ironically, it was my offer to work with Jamaal that stopped him from going in and requesting a leave of absence from Jerry Buss. I briefly tried to explain

Jamaal's situation to Jerry Buss, but he had already been filled with so much misinformation that truth was now not the issue.

The last thing Jerry Buss mentioned to me was that he hadn't gotten over the disappointment of losing our home opener against Houston. He wasn't having fun anymore coming to the games, and he wanted a new show. The defeat to the Houston Rockets deeply hurt all of us, but the truly excellent team rises above a bitter loss and plays better down the line. I felt confident we were doing just that.

We were on our way to another NBA championship. My final impression, as I left Buss's office, was that I felt sorry for him. I saw him as a man who was hustled by others into firing me for the wrong reasons. He was desperate to win big; he had listened to the whispers of unreliable confidantes and grumbling players; he had been suckered and didn't realize it.

After being fired, my drive home to Palos Verdes was one of disbelief. I knew there were no easy solutions to the predicament Magic Johnson caused with his demand to be traded, but I never thought I would be going home for dinner . . . jobless.

The moment she saw me, Cassie knew. I merely said, "It's over," and she knew what I meant. I then flicked on the TV to watch a live telecast of an announced press conference from the Forum. I had presumed that it was set up to cover the resolution of the Magic Johnson situation; instead, it was to announce my departure. It's scary watching your own viewing and burial from the living room with your family at your side. Within a couple of hours after the announcement, I received my first call from a fellow coach. It was Jack McKinney, who was responsible for getting me here in the first place. We had been through a great deal together, and now both had felt a great hurt connected with coaching the Lakers. His concern for my well-being, in light of the nightmare he had gone through, was a tremendous tribute to Jack and a great lift for me.

Soon after McKinney's call, I heard from Kareem, who wanted to voice his dismay at my firing. He told me he was not informed of this possibility. Not that he should have been, but I suspect other players, including Magic Johnson, were privy to front-office discussions to fire me. Kareem was angered at the way it was all handled and wanted to disassociate himself from being a part of this matter. It was a great source of satisfaction to know that the best player in the world knew you had done a good job and thought enough of you to call. Kareem and I had developed a mutual respect, and an impetuous firing could not shatter that bond.

Instead of speaking to the media throughout the evening, I decided to have one final press conference at the Forum. I felt proud of my time coaching the LA Lakers and did not want it to end being run out on a rail. There were too many good things that happened while coaching the Lakers. A world championship cannot be pushed aside by the whim of one person. We were such a great team, and I had a good relationship with the players. This positive connection was too strong for me to be bitter. I was deeply hurt by being fired but too proud of our team's achievements to let the memory turn ugly.

With these feelings, I went to the press conference wearing my championship ring. I had only worn it a few times, because it was so heavy, but today it was symbolic of all the good I had achieved in Los Angeles. Many of the media asked me if I was bitter toward Magic Johnson for forcing me out. I felt disappointed with his role in my dismissal but remembered the more rewarding days of working harmoniously together and enjoying the fruits of winning a world championship.

Later that day, I received a message that Pat Riley and Bill Sharman had called. I returned Pat Riley's call that evening just prior to the San Antonio game. I tried to be lighthearted for his sake, so I kidded him about already being 1-0 as a head coach since he took my place once when I was having surgery for my kidney stone. It took me over a week to return the call from Bill Sharman. I had mixed feelings about his role in my firing. I felt confident, through our three-year association, that Bill was very supportive of me and what I was doing. I had trusted his backing me, even though, at times, we disagreed on some trade possibilities.

Just in the past week, we had disagreed sharply on a trade of Nixon for Dennis Johnson. Bill was definitely for it, and I was against. But there was never a question in my mind of Bill's support of me as a coach. The confusion occurred when Jerry Buss told me his advisors were *unanimous* in getting rid of me. Buss said he called a meeting to discuss my status, and before any discussion, his advisors, Jerry West and Bill Sharman, told him there was no question in their minds—I had to go. This comment caused me a great deal of mental anguish and confusion, because I would have bet on Sharman voting to keep me and straightening out the problem with Magic.

During the week following my dismissal, I pondered my feelings toward Sharman. He was my friend; how could he vote in favor of this decision? When I finally called, I decided not to confront him with this single question, "Why did you vote me down?" I felt, at that time, that nothing could be gained except Bill feeling bad that I was disappointed in him. My guess into this matter is that Sharman probably didn't vote me down during their discussion on what was wrong with the team but that he wasn't strong enough in fighting for me to fend off the wolves. I needed him to take a firm stand, and what I got was "no comment." So our discussion was centered on some of the reasons why I was fired rather than on his involvement.

Bill said a major reason for my release was my inability to handle the super ego of the pro athlete. In their opinion, I was not adept at stroking the star despite the problems he may present. Their specific references were to Spencer Haywood, to Jim Chones, and very recently to Magic Johnson. In the cases of Haywood and Chones, I felt as though the proper decisions had been made. I was fair in handling them according to their demonstrated ability to help the team win. They became unhappy and, in my evaluation, were not players whose ability and contribution to the team demanded me to soothe their egos. To be blunt, they were not stars. Clearly, if they were not going to blend with the program, the smartest thing to do was to replace them with others who would be happy to play a supporting role.

I respected Bill Sharman tremendously, but I believed his assessment of my coaching was way off. I had always, and have always, been able to work well with stars, whether they were Ken Durrett, Kareem, and Magic or, later, Hank Gathers and Diana Taurasi. In fact, most people would tell you that Kareem would be the most difficult basketball star to deal with, period. But he and I had a terrific working relationship, and it is no exaggeration to say he was my strongest ally among the Lakers players.

Sharman said the organization, and Buss in particular, was still upset with the Kupchak-Chones deal. For the moment, I was the fall guy for all the downside of the deal. We were being criticized for not having an adequate backup center, and Buss's response was to say that I had made him give up Chones. We had gotten a couple of subpar games from Kupchak—namely, the infamous home opener against the Houston Rockets—and I had been the one who pushed the deal the hardest.

I told Sharman that someday the Lakers would put up a plaque in the Forum praising me as the one who brought about the Kupchak-Chones deal. As long as Mitch Kupchak remained healthy, I felt confident that deal would bring the Lakers to the NBA finals and perhaps another championship. To be criticized for not putting up with Spencer Haywood and Jim Chones was something I could openly accept, because I felt as though I had done the right thing.

The case of Magic Johnson was qualitatively different. He, too, had a super ego that needed to be soothed, but unlike the others, Magic could really play and win games. Magic's ability to deliver for his team demanded special consideration by me in dealing with his ego. I recognized that and had worked at achieving an understanding. There were times in practice, for example, when Magic would be awful. He would run drills in slow motion and disdain necessary repetitions. I would not take issue with him on such instances, because of his performance on the court when the lights were on. The bottom line was that Magic Johnson played hard for his team. My formula was, if you have an ego in need of understanding, then you better deliver wins for your team.

Magic Johnson scored high in both ego and winning performance, and therefore, I was prepared to deal with him. The irony of the Magic Johnson conflict was that there was no actual conflict. We had a good relationship for three seasons. It was not one of daily discord that finally broke wide open with Magic's demand to be traded. It was much closer to a relationship of understanding and mutual respect. What went wrong with this relationship, I can only guess. I know one thing for sure—Magic Johnson and I did not have violent differences inevitably leading to his outburst in Salt Lake City.

There were other influences outside my dealings with Magic. He was still feeling the effects of his knee surgery. I think he knew the leg wasn't the same yet, and he couldn't do it all as before. Magic was afraid he might not be able to perform as well. This contributed to his lashing out when things didn't get off to a great start. I am convinced that Magic felt as though the world would come down on him if he didn't personally lead the Lakers to another world title. The shock of losing to Houston and the memory of the miniseries embarrassment sent Magic into near panic. He was now in search of a reason for the failure. It wasn't going to be him. It couldn't be his teammates, like Norm Nixon, because he used them as the reason for failure last year, so it was going to be me.

In retrospect, I felt as though Magic made an impetuous remark out of frustration for being called out. I felt as though Magic had placed enormous pressure on himself to produce showtime, and when it wasn't happening immediately, he pushed the button and cried, "We need a change."

The day after my dismissal ended with a whopping victory by the Lakers over the San Antonio Spurs. The funeral ceremony seemed complete. Still, I kept waiting for the phone to ring telling me it was all a mistake and to hurry back to work.

The second day after the firing, I had to call the Forum to arrange a car deal through the Lakers' group ticket manager. He was not there when I called, so his secretary asked if he could return my call. When she asked me to spell my last name, I knew it was all over. After three years of being the head coach of the internationally famous Los Angeles Lakers, I had been forgotten in two days.

16

The Long Run

I decided to start a new life. I was not going to submit to my executioners. I was going to live and rise above this premature demise. I decided to read, to write, to run long distances, and in that way stay alert and fully alive for the next coaching opportunity. I sat down and made a list of things I had always wanted to do but had never found the time.

One was to write a book. I had been thinking about it for a few years. Now I would do it. The process of writing was painful, because it brought up, in microscopic detail, all the thrills and disappointments of my life in Los Angeles. I relived every step on the way to the final moment of being an orchestra leader in search of a band. I was a talented coach in the prime of my career without a team.

To ease the pain of recalling my Lakers experiences, I launched an extensive long-distance running program. I started running ten miles a day with the ultimate goal of completing a marathon. The running kept me in good spirits during the long days of winter. The aches of a long run were welcomed compensation for the absence of basketball activity.

I was advised to run twenty miles in preparation for the Long Beach Marathon. I did the twenty-mile training run and collapsed minutes later. I failed to drink any liquids during my run and paid the price with severe dehydration. My body went tilt; every part of me was in rebellion. Between the vomiting and diarrhea, I could barely stay conscious. Cassie took me to the hospital for immediate intravenous feeding to replace needed fluids. Within a few hours, I was fine, and the next day, I was ready to continue my training. I finally ran the Long Beach Marathon on my forty-third birthday and finished with a respectable time of three hours and forty-three minutes.

The highlight of my experience occurred during the twenty-fourth mile. I encountered severe stomach cramps that doubled me over and forced me to stop. I knew I wanted to continue, but the pain was unbearable. Just then, a fellow participant in a wheelchair came up behind me and shouted, "Come on buddy; bring it on home!" That was all I needed to hear. If this courageous man could handle the pain, I certainly could cope with my minor ache. It also reminded me that my present coaching situation was nothing in comparison to the hardships of others. My fellow marathoner gave me the courage to finish the race and, more importantly, to get on with my life. I saw very clearly that I was going to overcome my present situation and return to a successful coaching career.

Well, a coaching career.

A few months later I was hired to coach the Chicago Bulls. I was glad to be back in the NBA, though there would have been a lot better places to land. Understand that this was a Bulls team that was still two years away from drafting Michael Jordan. The talent level of the Bulls team I coached? Well, put it this way: With the Lakers, when the game was on the line, I got the ball to Kareem Abdul-Jabbar, the NBA's all-time leading scorer. With the Bulls, we gave it to Quintin Dailey, who averaged 14 points a game over his NBA career.

In a way, I do owe a debt of gratitude to the Bulls. Because they lost a coin flip to the Lakers in 1979, it was LA that ended up with the first pick in the draft, which ended up being Magic Johnson. The Bulls picked second and got David Greenwood.

It was a bad season all around in Chicago. We lost our first three games and were basically out of the playoffs by early December when we had a record of 6-13. It was about that time that anonymous comments critical of the job I was doing started appearing in the local papers from someone inside the organization. That someone turned out to be none other than

Rod Thorn, the team's general manager. I don't know—maybe he was still bitter that he was the one who had chosen heads in 1979. Whatever the case, I was let go after one season.

I went back to Palos Verdes to recharge for my next coaching position. During the morning, I would go to my makeshift office in my house and make phone calls, searching for jobs. I discovered that people who normally returned my phone call suddenly didn't—an early sign of a coach who has lost value in the basketball world. I was not easily discouraged. When reaching out to someone in the basketball community, I had a three-strike rule: I'd call three times, and if there was no response, I would strike you off my list and move on.

My old teammate at St. Joseph's, Jim Lynam told me not to get discouraged: "You only need one job. It only takes one person to love you." Well, there were many days when no one in the coaching world loved me.

On a whim, I went to see the president of Marymount College in Palos Verdes. Dr. Tom Wood invited me to discuss my future. He had a teaching opening in the English department but nothing in basketball. Marymount is a small college. How small? They didn't have a gym . . . *or a team.*

Dr. Wood wanted to help me and suggested that I start a new basketball team. I finally found someone to love me. I accepted the teaching and coaching position. I announced tryouts for basketball, and eight students showed up in the parking lot that had a basket at one end. After a few sessions in the parking lot, we picked up a math teacher and the son of the campus gardener, who preferred playing hoops to trimming the bougainvillea.

From there, we went two days a week to a recreational center in San Pedro, and the fast break was alive! We ran the speed game up and down the court for two hours of practice. We had no substitutes, so everyone was fully extended. We were game ready but had no games. I spent my free time calling small colleges in California, trying to schedule games, but that was for next year. During my first season at Marymount College, our only setback was when Manuel, the gardener's son, had to work or Rick, the math teacher, had to grade papers. Still, it was my one and only undefeated season.

Coaching at Marymount College helped me get an interview for the coaching job at Loyola Marymount University. No matter how slight my

Marymount College position was, it was always better to have a job when seeking a new one. I was interviewed by LMU and believed that I had a good chance to get the job. Five years before, I had been the head coach of the Los Angeles Lakers, and we practiced at the LMU court. I hoped my professional background would get me the job. Unfortunately, my friend Jim Lynam, the former LA Clippers coach, was selected. I heard that it was because he was "hot" in the basketball world, and I was not.

Well, except in Collegeville, Pennsylvania, home to Ursinus College. The people there thought a lot of me and offered me the opportunity, once again, to both teach and coach. They gave me a month to think about it. I loved the idea of being able to teach again but was getting some pushback from my family, who had gotten used to Palos Verdes, which is simply one of the most beautiful spots on earth. Particularly adamant about not relocating was my daughter, who kept repeating that she would not be attending "Uranus College."

As it turned out, she was right. A few days before I was due to give Ursinus my decision, I got a call from Lynam, who told me he was already resigning from LMU, before coaching a game, to take an assistant job with the Philadelphia 76ers. No one knew yet. Armed with this intel, I called LMU and told them I was interested in the opening but was also two days away from taking another job. They told me they'd get back to me, which they did soon after, and they invited me in for an interview.

Suddenly, someone loved me. I got the job.

In my first year at LMU, I began to insert the fast break offense with my new team. Eventually, our players would feel as if this was the only way to play the game. It became second nature to them. They would watch college basketball on TV and say how dull and boring it looked. My LMU players came to believe that the only way to play basketball was with the system—shoot the ball every five seconds and then press on defense and make the opposition shoot the ball in five seconds. Once that pattern was established, we knew the ultimate outcome of the game; we were going to win, because no one could play at that pace, except us.

There were times when we would go down 20 points in the first half and come back and win by 20 points in the second half. Therefore, a 40-point turnaround was not a big thing for us. We knew that a fast pace, an ultrafast pace, was our friend and that it would deliver by the final buzzer.

During that first season, we had a game with UCLA at Pauley Pavilion. They were the big boys from the west side, the school with more NCAA titles than anyone else; we were the little Jesuit school about to get beat up. In the first half, we were running the fast break and were surprisingly close. My only freshman, Enoch Simmons, was getting open shots in the speed game but missing; at halftime he was 2 for 13.

In the locker room, my assistant Jay Hillock said we could win this game if I were to tell Enoch to stop shooting, making it the biggest win of our season. I said no and told Enoch to keep shooting. The system says, "If you are open, shoot it." I couldn't break the rules just to give us a better chance to defeat UCLA. It would have sent a message to our team that we could pick and choose when we decided to run and shoot, and my message, every day, was to run and shoot every play of every game. There is to be no second guessing; if you are open, shoot it.

Enoch went out and shot 3 for 15, and we lost. After the game, Jay Hillock wouldn't even look at me. In his heart, he believed that I lost a chance to beat UCLA to preserve my system. For that game, he may have been right, but for Enoch and the rest of the season, I was right.

We had a game in Reno against the University of Nevada. It was mid-season, and we had already produced some high-scoring games. Our reputation had spread, so Reno was ready for us. The morning of the game, I overheard a conversation in our hotel lobby between two guests. One asked, "What brings you to town?" The other responded, "The circus; Loyola Marymount's basketball team plays here tonight."

I grinned and thought about our high-wire act. Early in the game, Nevada was running and gunning with us. They were outscoring us, and the crowd was ecstatic. The circus was in full swing. We are down by 10 points at halftime, and my players were in a full sweat. I asked them, "Are you a little spent from the frenetic pace of the game?" They nodded affirmative. I then said, "Well, if you're tired, how do you think the Reno players are feeling?"

We went out and scored the first 18 points of the second half. Nevada called a time-out, and our trainer, Chip Shafer, who never spoke to me about strategy, tapped me on the shoulder and said, "TMF, TMF, TMF." I was trying to be polite and ignore him, but he insisted, "TMF." So I said, "What the hell is TMF?" Chip pointed down at the Reno players, staggering out on the court, and said, "TMF is temporary muscular failure. They can't walk." Even though there was still plenty of time left, the game was over. Reno had come out too fast, and the pace destroyed them.

It's like running a marathon and going too fast the first 10 miles of the 26.2-mile trek. You can't recover, and the task of finishing, let alone winning, is almost impossible. We won the game by a large margin, and the circus packed its bags for the next stop.

We won enough games that first season to be selected for the NIT post-season tournament, with our first game at the University of California, Berkeley. Normal procedure is to send the weaker team away, while the power team plays at home. We walked into trouble at Cal's Harmon Gym, where a full house stood and yelled the entire game.

We ran our fast break and kept the score close. Enoch Simmons had six open jump shots and made five of them, never hesitating despite the pressure of the crowd. Since the UCLA game, Enoch learned that if they passed him the ball, he would shoot it.

The Cal game was also a clear example of how my system only really works with a total commitment from the players. Never was that more evident than with my center, Fred Bradford.

In my system, the center has to be an expert at taking the ball out of bounds on made baskets by the opposition. He must take the ball out of the net and pass to our point guard racing down the court in a half second. Most basketball teams believe the outlet pass is a routine skill that any player can do reasonably well without any training. In my system, the No. 5 man, the center, must be a skilled worker who will deliver the outlet with precision over and over again.

Perhaps the best example of this was my No. 5 man at George Mason, Mike Sharp, who executed the outlet pass to perfection. Mike was almost robotic in his execution of the outlet. Over and over in practice and in games, the ball was in the No. 1 guard's hands in a split second. How locked in was Mike? In a game against James Madison University, Mike took the ball out after the opposition scored and made the outlet pass. He then sprinted down the court to get an offensive rebound. As he got to the basket, the shot went in, and Mike proceeded to immediately grab the ball out of the net and pass it in to our No. 1 guard, who caught it and dribbled to half court before the officials finally whistled the play dead and tried to figure out what just happened.

During my first season at LMU, we made Fred Bradford our No. 5 man. Fred was a returning senior who had limited basketball talent, but he was a hard worker who would do anything for the team. Taking the ball out to start the offense was an honor for Fred; scoring points was not an issue for him.

Against Cal our fast break was generating lots of points. Fred quickly inbounded the ball on every Cal-made basket. After that, Fred unselfishly sprinted down the court for a possible open shot, of which there were none, or to get an offensive rebound, from which, so far, he had come up empty.

With less than a minute to play, Cal scored a free throw to go up a point. We did not call a time-out, as most teams would do, and had Fred snap the ball inbounds to ignite our break. We pushed the ball up quickly with our point guard, Keith Smith, who found our leading scorer, Forrest McKenzie, open on the right side in the No. 2 spot.

As Forrest caught the ball and released the shot, Fred was at half court sprinting to rebound the shot. Cal surrounded the basket, hoping for a miss, so that they could rebound the ball and win the game. The ball hit the rim and bounced high. As he had done the entire game to no avail, Fred Bradford came flying down the lane for the missed shot. The ball seemed to jump into his outstretched hands, and he followed with a two-hand dunk. Game over. Silence in Harmon Gym.

After countless efforts to sprint for a rebound, Fred Bradford made his only basket. Most basketball players only go hard when they think there is a good chance they will be rewarded with scoring. Fred Bradford went hard because it was his role in the fast break system. He did it without thinking. He did it instinctively, because that's what a No. 5 man does.

THE SYSTEM MIGHT have lost to UCLA, but it was in high gear to beat Cal, 80-75. We ended up going 19-11 that season, capping a record turnaround for the LMU team, which had gone 11-16 the season before.

And things were about to get better. Much better.

During the spring of my first year at LMU, I learned of personnel problems at USC (University of Southern California). Stan Morrison, their head coach, had been fired, and there were rumors of a big shake-up and that the players were unhappy. We were contacted by three different players who had an interest in transferring from USC to LMU. One call was from a former AAU (Amateur Athletic Union) coach of Tom Lewis, a high school All-American who was now a freshman at USC. Coming out of Mater Dei High, Lewis had all the credentials of a future NBA player: he was six feet seven, strong, quick, and an excellent scorer. The coach wanted to set up a meeting to evaluate our mutual interest.

My assistant coach who received the call, said we'd get back to him shortly to set up a time. On that same day, we received another call saying both Hank Gathers and Bo Kimble were interested in talking about transferring. I was only vaguely aware of them, but my assistants told me they were talented freshmen from my hometown of Philadelphia. We told them we'd get back to them shortly to discuss a possible meeting as well.

We then met as a coaching staff to discuss this unusual situation. Here we were struggling to recruit mediocre high school players who wouldn't give us the time of day, and now we had three very talented and highly sought-after players interested in coming to LMU.

I was all ears, listening to my assistants' evaluations, because I wouldn't have known any one of them if they walked through the door. So the debate was, how serious were any of the three about actually coming to LMU? They obviously had other choices. How would we decide on whom we went after? Could we get one, two, or all three? My assistant, Judas Prada, answered that last question by saying we couldn't get all three because the Philly guys wouldn't go with Lewis. So it was either two or one. I had also heard that some of the interest in LMU for Hank and Bo was because of a mutual friend from Philadelphia, Father Dave Hagen.

Father Dave was the grammar school coach and mentor for Hank and Bo and many of their North Philadelphia friends. His word was gold because of his kindness to the neighborhood kids. My connection to Father Dave went back to 1980 when we had just won the NBA championship with the

Lakers. Cassie asked me to donate a couple of scholarships to a summer camp I had run in the Pocono Mountains outside Philadelphia. Her best friend, Sister Mary Ellen Sheridan, was working with underprivileged kids in North Philly, and Sister Mary Ellen's friend Father Dave Hagen had some boys who would love to go to camp but didn't have the money. We sent two of Father Dave's boys to camp, and I thought that was the end of it. As it turned out, one of the boys, nicknamed Heat, became the point guard of the Dobbins Tech Philadelphia High School championship team with Hank Gathers and Bo Kimble. Because of the connection, when Hank and Bo were searching for a new college, Father Dave told them to go see Paul Westhead, because he would treat them fair and square.

I decided to recruit Hank and Bo and not Tom Lewis. It was an unusual situation, calling back and saying thanks but no thanks to a local high school superstar who, at the time, was thought to be the best of the USC players. My decision to recruit Bo Kimble and Hank Gathers changed LMU and my coaching career forever. They were the reason the speed game broke onto the national scene. Like George Barton from Cheltenham High School, Bo and Hank made my career. Their performance allowed us to lead the nation in scoring for three consecutive seasons. Once again, the fast break system was sound, but players made the difference. Bo and Hank were the tipping point to scoring 122 points per game. I was to be the bandleader along for the ride, a very fast ride.

17

I Told You So

When Hank Gathers and Bo Kimble made their visit, we showed them around campus, meeting students and faculty. Our academic dean was impressed with their classes, one being Russian. Both players had taken the class, but neither attempted to speak any Russian, a clear sign of Philly street smarts.

Later in the visit, we showed them some game films of our fast break style. They saw the rapid style of play up and down the court with frequent scoring. As we left the film room and were walking to the parking lot, Bo put his arm on my shoulder and said, "Coach, you're from Philly; we're from Philly. Don't bullshit us with this made-up video of your team's fast break. Nobody runs that fast." I had to convince him that it was actual game footage with no editing. Both Hank and Bo had a startled expression and said, "Count us in."

To seal the deal, I offered to make sure they were roommates next season. Bo spoke up and said, "We are good friends, but we never want to be together." It was clear that Hank and Bo wanted space to do their own thing. During their stay at LMU, they had separate housing, separate classes, and separate friends. Even in preseason pickup games, Hank and Bo were always on opposite teams, and neither one would allow the other to win.

Fortunately, when it came to LMU basketball, they thrived on performing together. In our fast break there were plenty of shots, rebounds, and glory to go around for both. In consecutive seasons, each led the NCAA in scoring. Hank led in 1988–89, with 1,015 points scored, and Bo led in 1989–90, scoring 1,131 points.

Hank was driven to be the best basketball player in America. What he didn't have in natural talent, he made up for with limitless hard work. Hank didn't have a smooth release of his jump shot, but he had a fistful of slam dunks to win any game. His finesse game was okay, but his power game was unstoppable.

After Hank's first season at LMU, he was invited to the Olympic training facility in Colorado Springs. He was selected with thirty-five other players to represent the United States in the Pan American Games. To show my support of Hank, I went to see him during the tryouts. As I was entering the practice courts, a group of female volleyball players were leaving, hysterically laughing about the shooting form of one of the players inside. They didn't call him by name, but I knew instinctively it was Hank.

Sure enough, once inside, there was Hank Gathers in a shooting drill, and he was missing most of his shots. He later told me he was struggling all week with his outside shooting but was playing harder than anyone in the camp.

Hank didn't make the select team that summer. He came home upset, somewhat embarrassed but determined to be the best college player in America. The next season, Hank led the NCAA in both scoring and rebounding, with 426 rebounds. He was only the fifth player in college basketball history to do both in the same season.

With his determination and physical power, Hank dominated games. With the ball, he would power to the basket, challenging anyone to stop him. Without the ball on offense, he would attack the rim on every shot. Hank felt that every missed shot by a teammate was an opportunity for him to score; he was like Cookie Monster, devouring every shot bouncing off the rim. The fast break system opened the door for offensive rebounds, and Hank took full advantage of the system. For most players, a few offensive rebounds were a good night's work; for Hank, 10 to 15 offensive rebounds wasn't enough. He wanted every one of them.

In addition to his scoring and rebounding skills, Hank Gathers was a tenacious defender. He would deny his man the ball and shut the offensive player down. If Hank was guarding you, forget about getting the ball. Once, in practice, my assistant Jay Hillock suggested we pull Hank off his deny defensive position and have him help in the lane. I asked Hank if he could help with offensive drivers coming down the lane, and he responded, "Sure, I can help, or I can deny my man, but not both. Which one do you want?" Realizing he was correct, I chanted, "Deny, deny, deny."

Later after practice, I told Jay Hillock to stop giving me clever defensive ideas. Our system was simple: deny on defense, run on offense, and nothing in between.

On one occasion, though, Hank broke our deny defensive philosophy. We were playing Santa Clara in the conference finals, with the winner going to the NCAA tournament. We were up 1 point with five seconds left in the game. Santa Clara had possession and called a time-out. I instructed our team to pressure the ball out of bounds and deny the pass to any of the four players inbounds. Hank was playing the man out of bounds, and he said to me, "Do you want me to pressure him and deny the pass?" I said, "Of course, that's what we do."

Hank left the huddle not convinced of my strategy. Santa Clara ran a back pick at half court, freeing up a player for an open lay-up. There wasn't a defender within fifteen feet. With pressure on the ball, anyone could lob the pass for a winning basket. We were going to lose. Santa Clara knew my defensive system and had a play to beat it. As the passer was about to release the ball, Hank, on his own, stepped back off the sideline, jumped up, and intercepted the pass in midair, clutching it as time ran out. Game over. We won. Hank the Bank won another one for us.

My system took on a whole new dimension when, in my third season at LMU, I decided to experiment with full-court defense to speed up the opposition's time for each possession. Teams were countering our speed game by slowing the game down, by not shooting the ball until late in the 45-second shot clock. So no matter if we shot the ball in four or five seconds, the opponent would take forty-five seconds.

From the first practice in the 1987–88 LMU season, we drilled full-court defense. Not knowing anything about this approach, I told the defense to not let their man catch the ball. This meant not letting the other team inbound the ball after we scored a basket. This was a most difficult task, because you had to immediately find your man and deny him from getting a pass.

To be honest, I wasn't as sure about pressing, as I presented to my players. The fact was that I had thought about pairing a running offense with a pressing defense since the early 1970s but had been discouraged by others every time I floated the idea.

In the summer of 1972, I was working the Jack Ramsay Camp Canadensis Basketball Camp in the Pocono Mountains of Pennsylvania. We had Hubie Brown, coach of the Atlanta Hawks and New York Knicks, as a guest speaker. After talking to the young players at the camp, Hubie talked to me about his full-court defensive strategy. I was intrigued by it and asked if my fast break team could implement his pressing defense along with the speed offensive game? He looked at me like I was a crazy man and said, "Absolutely not! You can do the fast break or full-court pressure defense, but not *both*."

Like so many coaches, pretty much all coaches, Hubie reasoned that players could not have the energy to sustain the pace. To do either full-court defense or fast break offense takes a total commitment by the players, and to expect players to combine them is impossible. Both styles would suffer and ultimately fail.

Hubie stressed, stick to one and perfect that. Don't get greedy and try to press and run. I accepted his evaluation and dedicated my coaching style to be a fast break coach. My defensive strategy was to complement my fast break with half-court man and zone defenses that would conserve the energy of my players. Speed to the max was my offensive game; there was no room for defense to the max.

For fifteen seasons after meeting with Hubie Brown, I worked at being the fast break Guru, totally forgetting about full-court defense.

But by 1987 I knew I had to do something to protect my running game, so I did the unthinkable: I taught full-court, all-game press. Even then, after ten days of practice, my players found ways to get open and break the defense. Other than the classic coach's line, "try harder," to stop the inbound pass, I had no solution for my defenders.

To get help, I called John Robinson, then the head coach of the LA Rams, and asked if I could come down to Anaheim and pick his brain? He agreed, and a few days later I showed up with my list of defensive problems. Coach Robinson, hearing the issues, sent me to his defensive coordinator, Fritz Shurmur, for counsel.

There were three major problems: First, our defender was easily faked by the offensive player's first move; Shurmur's answer was to train the defender to not go for the first fake. The second issue was, when our defender got beat going long, he would turn to see the ball and then lose his man; Shurmur's solution was to stay on the offensive receiver and, when he put his arm up to receive the ball, to close out the target and intercept the pass. The third and final issue was when the offensive player would go down the court and then circle back to the passer. In football they call this a button hook. Shurmur said when the offensive player does this, his players were directed to "destroy the target."

I returned to practice at LMU and told my players the three football rules. When I explained the third concept, I laughed and said that in basketball we don't "destroy the target." The concepts from the Rams' coaches vastly improved our defensive coverage. Our players had a new sense of confidence that they could deny the ball to the offense. We began to routinely ignore the first fake, and we learned how to close out the target and intercept or deflect the pass. We never practiced destroying the target, of course.

During the West Coast Conference championship game in 1988, Tom Lewis, now playing for Pepperdine, stole the ball at half court and was driving to the basket for an uncontested lay-up, when out of nowhere Corey Gaines appeared, trying to cut him off. As Tom Lewis left his feet to score, Gaines flew through the air and crashed into Lewis, knocking him ten feet into the stands. There was silence in the arena. Players, coaches, fans, and even the officials were stunned, not sure exactly what had just happened or what to do now.

During a lengthy time-out to make sure Lewis was okay and to determine what to do about the collision, I turned to Gaines and said, "What the hell did you just do?" He turned to me, a huge grin on his face, and said, "Destroy the target, Coach!"

The officials, still not certain of what they had just seen, gave Lewis two shots and the ball. We went on to win the game and advance to the NCAA tournament.

Looking back to the start of the season, I almost didn't go with the full-court defense. In fact, the day before our first game that season, my assistant coach, Judas T. Prada, said to me, "Now that we've practiced for thirty-eight days a full-court defense, let's get rid of this bullshit idea and play normal defense." I hesitated and then said, "We're going forward with the full-court defense in tomorrow's game."

The truth was, of course, that Judas was right. I had no idea what I was doing, and it could easily become a bullshit idea. But it didn't. Our new full-court defense, not our offense, was going to make all the difference.

That same season, we traveled to Santa Clara University to play our Jesuit rivals. There was no love lost between the schools or the coaches. Carol Williams, the Santa Clara coach, disliked me for bringing in transfer students and playing a wild style that broke the mold of how he believed basketball should be played.

We opened the game with our full-court deny defense, and Santa Clara countered by throwing the inbound pass over the top of our defender and then driving the ball for an easy score. We set the pace, but Santa Clara set the score, leading by 23 points in the first half. The good news for us was they didn't slow down and run their deliberate offense full of picks and screens. Carol Williams occasionally would shout, "Run the play," and the ball handler would look over and say, "But Coach, we have a three-on-one opportunity."

Things turned around in the second half when the Santa Clara players were too exhausted to keep the pace. They started missing easy shots given by our deny defense. Our team, because we did it every day in practice, was able to sustain the speed game and win the game. Our players never worried about being down 20-plus points; they knew the opposition would crack and that we would keep the fast pace.

I had stumbled into an offense and defense that the opponent, no matter how talented, could not beat. The harder they tried to keep up, the harder they collapsed; sometime in the second half you could see it in their eyes. They didn't want to keep going up and down the court this fast anymore.

Our players treated an opponent's retreat as an open invitation to go faster. On one occasion we were playing a preseason game at LMU against Holy Cross University, a fellow Jesuit college. Their coach, George Blaney, was a friend of mine. George wanted to treat his team to sunny California in the winter, and we were happy to accommodate with our run-and-gun system.

With about ten minutes left in the game, we were over the 100-point mark and going to win the game. Still, Holy Cross had hung tough and was within 12 points. They didn't give up as many other teams did. After the game, I was talking to Coach Blaney, and he said, "They were done with eight minutes to go in the game." I said, "No, your team hung in until the very end. You should be proud of their effort." George said, "I'm not talking about my players, I'm talking about the officials."

All three of the referees stood still on the same spots for the last eight minutes of the game, exhausted from the pace. Frequently, officials for our games worried if they could keep up with the frantic pace. They could never settle in and get their bearings on the game situation. They were required to always be moving. One advantage we gained from this was, when taking the ball out of bounds after the opponent scored, we frequently threw the ball to our No. 1 point guard without actually taking the ball *out of bounds*. We were so quick and the pace was so fast that the official never saw the infraction. They were too concerned with trying to stay up with the pace of the ball. The officials were in survival mode; forget a few missed calls along the way.

Our opponents developed a few tricks of their own against us. One was the fake injury to stop play. During a high-scoring game with the University of Oklahoma, one of their players fell flat on the court as if he'd been shot. For no apparent reason he stayed motionless for five minutes. Their coach, Billy Tubbs, was out there encouraging him to stay down. The officials were helpless to start the game since there was an apparently injured player down on the court.

He finally got up and went to the bench . . . and was back in the game at the next dead ball. The Oklahoma team got a considerable rest and were able to keep up with the fast pace. Later in the second half, it happened again. Same player, same ground, no apparent reason. Another rest.

Oklahoma ended up winning the game since the extended stoppages hadn't allowed us to wear them down. The "injuries" had given them renewed strength.

We made the NCAA tourney in 1988 and were seeded to play the University of Wyoming in Salt Lake City. With a few days to prepare, I asked my assistant Jay Hillock how we should defend Eric Lechner, Wyoming's dominate center. Jay said with a smirk, "We should have talked about this October 15 at the start of practice, not March 15 at the end of practice."

So without any specific defensive plan to contain Lechner, we showed up to run our fast break and let the system wear them down. In the beginning, Lechner was having his way, going into the low post and scoring at will. On the bench, I looked over at Jay Hillock, and he said, "I told you so."

They were winning sizably in the first half, mostly due to Lechner's inside play. Then, with about a minute to go, we ran off 12 straight points. We scored, stole the inbounds pass, and scored again. We did this over and over without Wyoming ever being able to get down on the offensive end for Lechner to go inside and score.

As the first half ended, it was obvious that the Wyoming players were stunned by the speed of the game. In the second half there was more of the same, fast break after fast break. Lechner was so tired that he staggered into the low post and didn't ask for the ball to score. The final score was LMU 119, Wyoming 115, the highest combined total in NCAA tournament history. We never found a way to stop Eric Lechner, but the system did find a way to wear him out.

As it turned out, that decision changed everything. The fast break was twice as potent because of the defense. It was like throwing gasoline on a fire.

Our fast break offense and full-court defense was in full swing during the 1988–89 season. We were first in the country in scoring, averaging 112 points per game. Teams in our conference were trying all kinds of tricks to slow us down. A common one was to put up new nets on the baskets just before the game. The tighter nets would hold the ball going through the basket and therefore slow down the speed of our outlet pass and, ultimately, our offense.

Routinely, the day of the game, before our shootaround practice, we would have our student manager stand on a table and stretch out the new net at each end of the court. By game time, the nets were wide enough to allow the ball to fly out of the basket and into the hands of our No. 5 man taking the ball out for the fast break.

A more serious threat to slowing us down were teams that managed to break our full-court press and still refused to shoot easy shots. They would hold the ball for the entire shot-clock possession. The best at controlling the pace of the game was Coach Lynn Nance of St. Mary's College.

St. Mary's and LMU both belonged to the West Coast Conference, so we played each other at least twice a season. In the 1988–89 season, St. Mary's was leading the NCAA in fewest points scored by opponents, while we were leading the NCAA in most points scored. The question became whose philosophy was going to prevail—fast or slow? Would the score be in the 100s or the 50s?

As the game rolled into the second half, we were comfortably ahead by 18 points, with five minutes to go. I started to freely substitute my stars, Hank Gathers and Bo Kimble, so that the subs could enjoy the fun of playtime. Normally, as the game clock winds down with the score out of reach, the opposing coach subs freely also. The last three minutes becomes second team versus second team, and you just let the clock run out with little regard to who is doing what.

Coach Lynn Nance, however, decided to keep all his starters in the game against my second team and also continued to hold the ball for the entire shot-clock possession. There was no attempt to take advantage of an easy score but rather an attempt to keep the total score down. Realizing the strategy, I countered by putting my starters back in the game. We were not going to allow them to hold the score down; we were going to run it up. After the game, Lynn Nance refused to shake hands because of my tactic. Normally, I would never have my first team in at the end to run up the score, but I felt entitled to do so when St. Mary's was trying to keep it down. Their goal was to be first in defense, but our goal, just as important to us, was to be first in offense. We won the game, 150–119.

Hank Egan, of the University of San Diego, was another coach who believed that I was destroying basketball. Playing in San Diego, with the game well in hand for us, both teams had their second unit in the game to run out the clock. One of my subs, John Vergason, made a few mistakes in a row, and I called a time-out with a minute to go. My sole purpose was to give Vergason a piece of my mind; however, this late time-out felt like an insult to the losing team. It appeared to the home fans that we were rubbing it in.

During the time-out, as I was in the team huddle with Vergason, Coach Egan was glaring down at me. Without my knowledge, my son Paul, who was my grad assistant, glared back at Egan. If looks could kill, there would have been two dead guys on the court. Weeks later, I apologized to Coach Egan for my inappropriate time-out. He agreed that it was a stupid move but said he had a new-found respect for Paul. He admired the way he stood up for me. From that moment, a rivalry full of dislike became a friendship full of respect.

Being a coach is just like any other job. Some people in your profession are going to like you, and some are not. In coaching, the reasons for dislike usually are on a personal level—maybe someone doesn't like how you treated a friend of theirs or feels you ran up the score on them.

I may be unique in that there were coaches who didn't like me purely based on my style of play. Those coaches didn't just dislike my system, didn't just think it made a mockery of the game, but some had real fears that it had the potential to destroy basketball as they knew it. Of course, others just thought it made them look bad, even if they were beating it.

This latter group disliked the system, and me, because they quickly realized one of my central reasons for using it: it provided a method to beat superior talent. They didn't like that I wouldn't take my beatings like a good coach, wouldn't be happy with a handshake and a "your team played well," after getting trounced. They also hated that my style made them have to coach differently, that it had the potential of forcing their players to do things they either weren't accustomed to or had specifically been coached *not* to do.

Geno Auriemma, University of Connecticut's women's basketball coach, has the best team in America, year in and year out. His players show up ready to beat you, and they take no prisoners. If you try to play good fundamental basketball against Geno's team, you'll lose, 85–35, and he will congratulate you for working hard and playing the "right" way. If your team is under control, with their half-court, protect-the-basket defense and their methodical pass-and-screen offense, they will play a smart game but lose by 50.

My fast break system gives you a chance to beat the best. Run them on every possession, and fatigue will set in. Then you are in charge of the game. You control the outcome. The challenge now is not the talent of the enemy; it's the ability of your team to sustain the speed game.

When my Oregon women played Geno Auriemma's UConn team, we were ready to run the system for forty minutes. I was in the fifth and final year of my contract, and I had been brought in to infuse excitement into what had been a methodical, mediocre program. Oregon wanted fan interest, and my system promised speed and entertainment. I was unsuccessful in recruiting top-level women to our program, so winning games didn't come easy.

Anticipating that I would not have my contract renewed after the season, I decided to go all out in my fast break offense and full-court defense. In the preseason practices and games, we experimented with a new trapping defense, more aggressive and risky than any of my previous teams. The blitz defense set traps of two defenders on the ball for the whole possession. The result was either a steal and possession or a score by the opponent, which also resulted in a possession. The pace of the game was guaranteed to be fast.

We were 6-1 going into Hartford to play the defending national champions. Most teams playing against Geno try to control the tempo by holding the ball on offense and running a pattern play to the end of the shot clock; and then they miss the shot.

We did just the opposite. We ran the ball on offense and shot within five seconds; then we pressed full court and made UConn shoot within five seconds. I had convinced my players that we could pull off a major upset if, *if*, they followed the system and sustained it for forty minutes.

We showed signs of it working as UConn committed thirteen turnovers in the first half, a result of our trapping defense. But our fast break offense was sporadic. It was a back-and-forth, 10-point-margin game. We had them playing our style, but we failed to sustain the pace. UConn's superior talent soon began to take over, and my team began to crack.

The only player on my team who didn't was a freshman, Chrishae Rowe. She was a tough kid who didn't break down. She pushed the ball on offense faster than UConn could set their defense. Scoring 27 points was easy for Chrishae; getting my team to follow her lead proved impossible.

In the end, we were trampled, 118–68. Our total points were the most scored against UConn all season, and despite the 50-point loss, I knew we almost pulled off the upset. I succeeded in having my team run and press but failed to train them to sustain the system.

Even with a big win, Geno couldn't resist to get in a shot at my system and me.

"I don't even think that's schoolyard basketball," he told reporters after the game. "Where I grew up, if you played like that, you wouldn't be allowed to play anymore."

And of course, there was Hubie Brown. I crossed paths again with the guy who told me I couldn't both run and press, in the 1990s in Moscow during a basketball coach's clinic sponsored by the NBA. We were conducting on-the-court demonstrations to eight hundred of the top coaches in Russia, and I gave a defensive lecture on how to deny offensive movement by shutting down all passing outlets.

After following Hubie Brown's full-court pressure defense, I took it to another level and had my players attempt to deny the ball all over the court for the entire possession, for the entire game. Hubie went to Jack Ramsay and said, "Your boy, Westhead, is killing us with his wild defensive ideas. We're looking like dummies in front of the Russians!"

Hubie was appalled at my unorthodox style of telling the defender not to look at the ball but to face guard his man and prevent the pass. To Hubie's credit, sound defense always instructs the player to see his man and the ball. I taught players to see only the offensive man they were guarding. During our NBA coaches' clinic in Russia, we were hosted by the Russian delegation to a banquet-style dinner. I arrived a few minutes late and was separated from the other NBA coaches. Only Mike Banton and I sat together with other Russian coaches. As the different dishes were being passed around, shots of vodka were raised celebrating our arrival in Moscow. I don't like vodka, so I routinely threw it over my shoulder. Being totally sober and not distracted by Russian conversation, I noticed a dish of cooked chicken that looked blue. I said to my former St. Joseph's College player Mike Banton, "I am not eating this concoction." He agreed, and it was passed on.

Unfortunately, the U.S. coaches down at the other end were too polite and ate the blue chicken. The next day, every one of those coaches, Jack Ramsay, Jim Lynam, and Hubie Brown, were all sick from the banquet, saying they had been up all night and could not make today's coaches' clinic.

I went to the clinic prepared to do it by myself. Only famous coaches like Bobby Knight ever did one-man clinics. This was my chance to be a star. Halfway through my first clinic, who showed up but none other than Hubie Brown. He could barely stand up, but he also didn't trust me. Hubie may have been dying, but he would not let me destroy the NBA image for the Russian coaches.

I was doing my fast break clinic, demonstrating how to outlet the ball and pass ahead to my shooter in the right corner in three seconds. As the shot was in the air, I demonstrated how my other players attacked the basket to rebound the potential miss. Hubie jumped up and ran onto the court, screaming, "Triangle rebounding! Triangle rebounding!" He applauded my concept and sat back down. My teams did this all the time on every shot. I didn't know in the coaching trade this was triangle rebounding. Hubie thought it was a stroke of genius. I was happy for his grin of approval.

I suddenly realized that it wasn't the speed of the outlet pass or the speed of the player sprinting to designated spots or the speed of the shot going off in three seconds. It was the speed of the offensive rebounder flying to get the missed shot. In the final analysis, believe it or not, my fast break system is a *rebounding* system. That is why it works. We get our rebounders down in position before the defenders have a chance to block out.

And ironically, it was Hubie Brown who uncovered the key to my fast break. I'd thank him . . . but I'm not sure he'd want the credit.

18

No Plan B

By the 1989–90 season, the system we put in at LMU was operating at top gear. ESPN wanted to put us on national TV to show the run and gun. The opponent would be LSU featuring Shaquille O'Neal and Chris Jackson. ESPN slotted a Saturday noon game in Baton Rouge, but unfortunately, we had scheduled conference games Friday and Saturday on the same weekend. The solution was to play St. Mary's at home on Thursday night, travel to Louisiana on Friday, and play LSU at noon on Saturday. After the game with LSU, we'd then fly back to Los Angeles and play the University of San Francisco on Sunday. Three games in four days with extensive travel in between. We didn't think twice about the task. We were a running team, so we were confident we would never tire. Plus, we wanted the national exposure.

The St. Mary's game went as predicted, we won, 150–119, but the trip to Baton Rouge took longer than expected. We managed to get in a late afternoon workout in preparation for the Saturday noon game.

ESPN's announcer, Quinn Buckner, was grinning from ear to ear before the game, because he knew this was going to be a shootout. LSU's coach Dale Brown had been practicing all week for the fast break game, but nothing can get you ready to run for forty minutes. We started out by missing shots, and LSU took an early lead. Hank Gathers had his first five shots blocked by Shaq. During a TV time-out, Gathers huddled with the team and said, "Get me the ball!" Instead of shying away from another blocked shot, Hank took it right to the defense and scored. After an awful start, Hank ended up scoring 48 points and got thirteen rebounds.

In our fast break game, Gathers was unstoppable. LSU could not keep up the fast pace. They were bigger and stronger, but we were faster with more endurance. At one point in the game, an LSU player became so exhausted that he threw the ball into the seats just to stop play; he had to find some way to catch his breath.

At the end of regulation, the game was tied, 134–134. In overtime we were up 3 points and stole the ball. My shooting guard, Jeff Fryer, had the ball and was open to drive to the basket; however, he pulled up and took an open three-point shot, a shot he had been programmed to take in the system. He missed, and we went on to lose to LSU, 148–141.

Fans at the game said it was the best game ever played at the Maravich Assembly Center.

One hour later, we were on the long road back to Los Angeles for a game the next day. Everyone expected us to show up on Sunday tired, flat, with no run left in our game. That was a mistake. We came out full of energy and speed. Our LMU team ran the fast break system to perfection and cruised to an easy 157–115 victory. Instead of three games in four days breaking us, it ignited us. Once you have the speed game in your blood, nothing slows it down. The mighty Lions scored 448 points in those three games, an average of 149.3 points a game.

I have constantly looked for ways to improve the speed and endurance of my fast break teams. While at LMU, I took my team to Sand Dune Park in Manhattan Beach. These sand dunes go straight up for about one hundred yards. It is a difficult task to walk up the dunes let alone run. I tried it first myself and then felt confident the players could do it twice. Many of the players struggled to finish and fell back down to the ground. Bo Kimble got halfway and stopped, complaining that his knee was acting up. Later in the season, Kimble went back to the sand dunes and did it twice with his hands in the air.

The dunes became a badge of honor, proof that our team was the fittest in all of basketball.

We also tried some deepwater maneuvers in the pool at LMU. Players would wear life vests and do sprints in the deep end for thirty to sixty seconds and then repeat it over and over. Years later I took this technique to the Denver Nuggets and had my NBA players go from the basketball court to the pool. Things were going fine until Orlando Woolridge said he was breaking out on his face because of the chlorine in the water and produced a doctor's note saying he couldn't go in the water anymore.

A few days later, three more players came up with the same rash and notes from their doctors, saying no more swimming pool. I stopped the program for the team. Weeks later, I met the director of the pool at Regis College, where we had trained, and told him of our misfortune. He looked puzzled: "We don't use chlorine to clean our pool."

Years later, after my tenure with the Nuggets, I was named head coach at George Mason University to install the fast break system to the max. We were going to run on offense and press on defense and score in the 100s. The school's sports-information director labeled it Paul Ball, and I was committed to delivering. Training the team for the offense meant I had to come up with something new, though.

Without the sand dunes of Los Angeles and the swimming pools of Denver, I initiated parachute training in Fairfax, Virginia. We had our players strapped with parachutes to their backs and had them run hundred-yard dashes. The chute would open up behind them as they started their sprint, to create drag with the wind pulling the players back while they dug in to go forward. We were going to be the fastest basketball players in America.

The track coach at George Mason, John Cook, cautioned me that we were going too fast in our training, but I would hear none of it. In one of the practices just before the first game, my friend Bill Gavin came to observe. He knew nothing about basketball but everything about strategy. Bill had been Richard Nixon's speech writer during his presidential campaigns and was a genius, but not when it came to sports. After watching two hours of up and down, fast break, and full-court press defense, he asked, "If this Paul Ball doesn't work, what's your plan B?"

Bill quickly explained that every political operation has a backup plan, a plan B. I told him I had no plan B. I had never even thought of another way of playing. Bill left practice and said he would research if there had ever been any successful ventures without a plan B. Later, he told me he found one, and only one: Cortez.

Bill said that when Cortez marched into Mexico, he had a big party the night before a battle with the Aztecs. During the festivities, he had his men look out at the Pacific Ocean where their ships were moored. As they watched, he had all the ships torched and destroyed. He then pointed inland toward the enemy and said there was only one plan . . . forward!

That is how I felt. In my system, there was no going back. Whether on courts, in pools, over sand dunes, or with parachutes strapped to their backs, my players would always move forward. Fast.

In 1989-90 we had two monumental games in Philadelphia. I was bringing the system back to my hometown. As a player for Jack Ramsay, I was insignificant. My academic grade point average, 3.4, was higher than my points per game average, 2.1.

More importantly, I was bringing Bo Kimble and Hank Gathers, the pride of Dobbin Tech and North Philly, back home. This was also as Hank was learning how to cope with the medication for his heart condition.

All three of us Philadelphians wanted to win that weekend. The first game was at St. Joe's, my alma mater. The same gym I used to play in was full of eager Hawk fans screaming to see the fast break system, developed in Philly, crash and burn. We were not at our best. Hank was struggling to get up and down the court. With a few seconds remaining, St. Joe's tied the game with a free throw.

We ran the ball up the court, and Bo Kimble took a running jump shot at half court. And swish, we won at the buzzer. Still, our locker room was quiet; Hank was despondent. He had a bad game and was sprawled out on the floor, crying. He was embarrassed and didn't want to face his friends and family.

After the game at St. Joseph's, Hank Gathers was so distraught that he returned to the hotel, wanting to be alone. The other players were happy and wanted to celebrate. Hank wanted no part in that. His mom, Lucille, came to the hotel and collected the team's uniforms to clean them for the next game against La Salle. To isolate himself from family and friends, Hank came to my hotel room. He knew players weren't going to stop by and chat with their coach. Tomorrow at practice would be soon enough to see Coach Westhead. Hank knew that my wife, Cassie, was with me, and they were friends. They were in a history class together and shared ideas and study notes. For Hank, Cassie's room was safe. Most of the time in our hotel room, Hank was in the bathroom, finally alone. The next day at practice, Hank was full of life. He had gone home to his mom and returned with a smile and clean uniforms. Hank was back; he was in good shape. The game uniforms, however, were not. Our only away uniforms were now pink. In the washing, the colors blended and came out a new LMU pink. The team wore them as a badge of honor for Hank's mom.

The next day at practice, Hank was his old self. We had a crisp practice, and Hank was back leading the fast break. I knew he was going to explode with energy the next game against La Salle. In some respects, this was more of a city rivalry. Many of the players on the La Salle team played against Hank and Bo in high school. This was the game for bragging rights, and there was another full house in the downtown Convention Hall, where La Salle was undefeated.

During warm-ups, we heard a loud train whistle vibrating through the arena. It was introducing La Salle's All-American player, Lionel "the Train" Simmons, and the Explorers.

The game was vintage fast break offense and full-court defense. We'd score, and then they'd score. Over and over and over. Bo was draining jump shots, Hank was rattling the rim with dunks and rebounds, and Simmons was scoring at will. The outcome was going to be decided by which team could sustain the frantic pace. We knew we could; we always did.

But La Salle went stride for stride—that is, until the last two minutes, when they began to falter. Lionel Simmons missed some easy shots and could barely stand erect at the foul line for free throws. I almost felt sorry for this great athlete; the train had run out of steam.

On the other side, Hank was in full stride, leading LMU in our speed game. With seconds to go, Hank and Bo came out of the game glowing with joy. Home at last. After the game, La Salle's coach, Bill "Speedy" Morris, was not happy. He felt as though his team got suckered by a gimmicky style of basketball. Speedy felt that this wasn't basketball—it was street ball.

Well, for him it was a cheap trick, but for us it was a high-precision machine spitting out basket after basket endlessly.

19

No Sound

Now cracks a noble heart. Good-night, sweet prince; And flights of angels sing thee to thy rest.

—WILLIAM SHAKESPEARE, *Hamlet*

The same year that Hank and Bo transferred from USC, Corey Gaines transferred to LMU from UCLA. Early on, Corey came to me and said our fast break system depressed him, because he was going to beat everybody down the court on every possession. This made him depressed because Hank and Bo were his friends, and as the point guard, he would beat them all the time and not be able to feed them for shots.

I assured him that Hank and Bo would play faster and go with him. I have learned that no matter how fast the point guard dribbles, other players will fly with him. Sure enough, Gaines was a speed demon with the ball, and sure enough, the other four players were down court ahead of him ready to score. Without the perfect point guard, the fast break is doomed to fail. You can judge how your speed game is by the speed of the point guard. With the speed guaranteed, it was the physical and mental strength of Hank Gathers that made us win.

Hank would rebound the missed shot on defense outlet to Corey, giving him a head start, and then come flying down court, catching everybody.

Hank wanted to sprint the floor to score, but more importantly, he wanted to get every offensive rebound. We won most of our games not because of our outside shooting but because of Gathers flying down the lane and scoring on offensive rebounds. Hank the Bank owned the offensive glass. He wanted every missed shot.

One time in practice, we were running the break, and Corey passed ahead to an open No. 2 guard, Jeff Fryer. Four times in a row, Gaines passed to Fryer, who shot a three-pointer each time. Hank came rumbling down the court screaming at Fryer not to shoot again. Hank came to me and said, "Talk to Fryer; he's shooting all the time." I said, "Hank, when Corey passes to him, Jeff is told to shoot by me. However, when he misses, you, as the No. 4 man, are to come down the lane and rebound and score his miss." Hank nodded and said okay.

The next play, the ball went again to Fryer, who again shot. As he was releasing the ball, Hank came sprinting down the lane screaming, "Fryer, miss!" Hank didn't mind Fryer shooting; he just wanted him to miss and feed the Bank.

We traveled to Corvallis, Oregon, to play the Oregon State Beavers. It was the last game of a contract demanding we play two games at Oregon State and one game at LMU. We were the small program who had to do two for ones to get games with bigger basketball conferences. The Pac-10 was far superior to our West Coast Conference. We had to play this game without the services of Hank Gathers, who was being monitored for a heart issue after he collapsed during a game against UC Santa Barbara.

We were learning how to play without Hank, then the leading scorer and rebounder in the country. The system would be sorely tested without Hank the Bank. As it turned out, we ran the system to perfection. Oregon State decided to run with us, so it was forty minutes of nonstop up-and-down the court. We had lost the two previous games against the Beavers with the control coach Ralph Miller. Now with Jim Anderson at the helm, Oregon State decided to play the speed game; *our* game. They were confident that the fast pace would work well with their All-American guard, Gary Payton, who was spectacular, scoring 48 points.

But our guys thrived in this fast pace; it was just like practice. They could sense the outcome. Bo Kimble was on fire, scoring 53 points.

It all came down to the last possession. We had the ball with twenty seconds remaining in the game. During a time-out, we set up a play for Bo to catch the ball and shoot. As the teams walked out from their respective huddles, I overheard Gary Payton say to Coach Anderson, "Let me glove Kimble." Payton was a tenacious defender who took pride in shutting you down. The play developed, and we got it to Kimble, who drove and shot a running jump shot. Gary Payton stayed with Bo and forced a tough shot attempt. Bo Kimble's shot went in the basket, and Gary Payton was called for a foul—his fifth, disqualifying foul.

With a few seconds remaining, Payton went to the bench, getting a deserved standing ovation. It was Oregon State's only loss at Gill Coliseum that season, and we went home with another normal system win, 117–113. When every player believes in the running game, anything can happen. We won on the road and without our star player, Hank Gathers. The system became the star.

NOTHING WAS UNUSUAL about the day of the game against the University of Portland. We were rolling as we had been all season. In the West Coast Conference we had gone 13-1, winning our games by an average margin of 23 points. In the first round of the conference tournament, held at LMU's Gersten Pavilion, we had beaten Gonzaga 121–84. There was no reason to think that Portland would fare any better; we had beaten the Pilots by margins of 25 and 23 during the regular season.

We were the twenty-second-ranked team in the nation, playing at home to a full house. Everyone, including myself, the players, and our fans, was eager for us to play and advance, and in the first few minutes, you could tell that the system was clicking, as it had most of the season. Everything was working—press and run, press and run—when with about fourteen minutes left in the half, we stole the ball and passed it ahead to Hank, who went in for a slam dunk. He turned to get back on defense and collapsed at center court just two yards away from Portland guard Erik Spoelstra.

There was nothing leading up to that moment that would make you think a problem was about to happen. It wasn't like Hank wasn't right that morning or in warm-ups. Nothing. He was the same Hank as always.

I saw him fall and momentarily try to sit up and fall back down again. I don't know what I was thinking at that time. But I do remember that Gersten Pavilion was packed, standing room only, and yet there was an eerie silence, a hush. I don't mean quiet—I mean *no sound*.

An ambulance came, and Hank was taken outside. The team stayed in the locker room, and I went to the hospital, Daniel Freeman, after the ambulance left. In some respects, I felt the way I did when I drove to the hospital after Jack McKinney's accident, but then, I knew Jack was alive. Now, I had no idea about Hank.

I arrived to find Hank in a very small emergency room, lying down as if he were asleep. I knew then.

I WENT BACK to LMU and told the team. They hadn't heard yet—this was before cell phones. But they could tell from my expression the moment I walked into the locker room.

The only players that I had a relationship with as equals have been Kareem Abdul-Jabbar and Hank Gathers. Hank didn't see me as his superior; he saw himself as a major actor or player and me as a director who could facilitate his getting better. And he had. He had become one of the best and best-known players in the nation. And now he was gone.

I told the players I would leave it to them to decide if they wanted to continue playing that season. To be honest, they kind of took the decision from me, because they overwhelmingly said they wanted to go forward.

It was an honest decision on their part; for me, in my heart of hearts, I'm not sure what I would have done. It was such a difficult time; if someone had said the best way we could honor Hank was to pack it up and never play another game, I don't think I would have objected.

The beauty of the players was that they never made it seem like a Hollywood script; they clearly felt as though it was their way of honoring Hank. They were sincere and straightforward and went on to play at a high level in the tournament, because they no longer really cared about winning or losing. They were playing for Hank but did not equate that with winning; therefore, they played better. They didn't want to win for Hank; they simply wanted to perform for him.

20

I Know

We were selected to play in the NCAA tournament as a twelfth seed. Everything in life was confusing. After Hank's death, everything seemed insignificant, except basketball. The players wanted the game to help cure the hurt. Basketball was the one thing that made sense in their life. Practice was quiet and efficient. Players ran the fast break for a release of the pain inside—no rah-rah, no bickering, just hard play over and over. We had one fling of emotion in practice, when Terrell Lowery took a swing at John O'Connell for no reason. It was raw emotion unleashed, and it was over in a second.

Terrell was a freshman and was close to both Bo Kimble and Hank Gathers. They would try and persuade Terrell, as a point guard, to pass them the ball in the fast break. Terrell was a little reindeer learning how to run with the herd. Hank was his leader, and when he called for the ball, Terrell wanted to please. With Hank gone, Terrell felt the hurt of the missing leader.

After a few practices, we were off to the Long Beach Arena for the first round of the NCAA playoffs. From LMU it is fifteen miles down the 405 freeway to the game. The odds were that we would lose the game and make the short ride back home. My assistant coach, Judas Prada, was so sure we would lose that he brought one suit for our game against New Mexico

State; that was it, laughing at the rest of us who brought more clothes for possible future games.

The game was standing room only. Not only did people want to see us and our system, but they wanted to say goodbye to Hank. If we were going to win, the scoring burden would rest on Bo Kimble. He was leading the nation in scoring, but he now had to add Hank's points to his total.

Early in the New Mexico State game, Bo picked up a couple of personal fouls. The standard rule of thumb is to take your player out when he gets his second personal in the first half. I never followed that standard, just as I never followed many other rules for acceptable basketball. We were pirates who thrived on breaking rules.

Then Bo picked up his third foul with ten minutes remaining in the first half. I didn't even flinch; Bo stayed in the game. Now, even the LMU fans were nervous. "Take Bo out, take Bo out" was their plea. Sure enough, they were correct. Bo Kimble picked up his fourth personal with five minutes remaining in the half.

Our fans were beside themselves. I took Bo out of the game. They frowned at my late decision. I sat Bo down next to me and said, "You have four fouls." He said, "I know." I said, "Well, go back in now and don't foul." At the scorer's table Bo waited to go back into the game with a New Mexico State player who said to him, "Your coach is one crazy dude." Bo replied, "I know."

My reasoning for putting Bo Kimble back in the game was that he had 7 points. We needed him to score much more, and he wasn't going to achieve that sitting next to me. Bo played the rest of the game without fouling out and scored 45 points in a 111–92 victory.

Sometimes you break the standard rules to win. During the New Mexico State game, Bo was fouled going to the basket. He had previously announced that he would shoot his first free throw left-handed in honor of his Philadelphia friend and teammate, Hank Gathers. During his career, Hank struggled with free-throw shooting. Even though he had led the NCAA in scoring and rebounding in his junior year, Hank decided to shoot left-handed for his senior year. With modest success, Hank went to the line, game after game, shooting free throws left-handed.

Bo Kimble now was determined to pay tribute to his fallen friend with this symbolic shot. With the excitement of our first NCAA tourney game, I had forgotten Bo's promise. Now, right in front of our bench, it was about to happen. Our fans were suddenly silent as Bo stepped to the line. Players on the bench grabbed hold of each other for support. All of a sudden, time had stopped. Bo had the ball cupped in his left hand, gentle like a bird about to fly for the first time. The shot was for Hank. The ball was all our memories of Hank. The shot went up in the air. The ball went in; Hank was in. For the moment, we were safe.

OUR SECOND-ROUND GAME was against Michigan, champions from the previous year. Steve Fisher took over the coaching in the postseason and hadn't lost a game yet in the NCAA postseason play. Once again, we were the underdogs against a Michigan team with four eventual first-round NBA draft picks. In the locker room, I told the players to believe in the system; run and shoot, run and shoot, it would prevail. Our players were so focused on play that they just wanted the game to start. To our players, everything was about play. Play to remember Hank; play to forget Hank.

Before the game, I met the officials, and the lead referee was John Clougherty, who had officiated the championship game last year. It was Clougherty who called a controversial foul against Seton Hall in the final seconds. Michigan's Rumeal Robinson made a free throw to win the championship. Seton Hall's coach, P. J. Carlesimo, was very kind in saying it was the correct call. I wouldn't have been so gracious.

I was worried we might get more of the same Michigan favoritism. Fortunately, our players couldn't have cared less about coaches and referees. They wanted to play. The Michigan team was ready for the speed game. Even though their coach, Steve Fisher, warned them not to get into a running game with LMU, the Michigan players embraced the style. With their talent, they could thrive in a fast pace. They were the superior athletes. It made no sense to slow down and be conservative.

Ten minutes into the game, the run-and-shoot style was working for both teams. Michigan was showing why they had future NBA players on their team. Rumeal Robinson, their point guard, was leading the excitement.

He was a four-year veteran who knew how to win a championship. Late in the first half, Terrell Lowery stole the ball and drove in for a lay-up. After the basket, when Rumeal Robinson took the ball to inbound the offensive play, Terrell jumped up next to him, denying the pass. Terrell Lowery was a street fighter from Oakland challenging the experienced Robinson.

It sent a message to the Michigan team—there may be more than fun waiting for them in this run-and-shoot contest. Terrell Lowery and the LMU Lions were determined to play this frantic style for forty minutes. Michigan began to wonder if they could last. At halftime, with each team scoring well into the 70s, there was no going back. Both teams were in for the speed game, and now it was hard to put the brakes on.

Our team was very comfortable at this pace and knew it was over for Michigan. Despite their talent, they couldn't keep it up. They came out too fast and could not regain their strength. An inexperienced marathon runner who starts too fast is done at mile thirteen, with half the race remaining. Likewise, Michigan would now pay the price for running with us early in the game. As they began to wilt, we got stronger. Jeff Fryer, our three-point specialist, continued to drill shots. Jeff Fryer would end up making eleven three-point shots to set the NCAA tournament record.

For us, it was like practice; for Michigan, it was hell. Their players were barely standing at the final buzzer. The final score, 149–115, showed that talent can't beat a run and shoot that never slows down. On that day, in Long Beach, California, the fast break system was unbeatable. Executing the system for a full game will always win.

WE WERE NOW in the NCAA Sweet Sixteen. No one expected us to advance past the first round, and now we are going to Oakland to play Alabama. They were big and strong; it would be men versus boys. Our only hope was to outrun them, as we had with Michigan.

Their coach, Wimp Sanderson, had vowed to slow the game down. The night before the game, Cassie and I went out to dinner with the Sandersons. We didn't talk about basketball, but all night Wimp had a silly grin on his face. He acted as if he had a surprise for me and my team. Early in the game it was obvious that Alabama was going to run down the shot clock on every possession. We were not going to be able to get them in a run-and-shoot game. Their power and strength inside would cancel out our speed. No matter what we did defensively to speed up the game, Wimp would not allow his team to bite.

We were able to score on some defensive steals by sending four players to attack the ball in the full court. Even when it didn't work, Alabama didn't take advantage of the three-on-one offensive opportunities. Our players became frustrated with the slow pace but managed to keep the lead throughout the game. Fast breaks were few, but our shooting percentage was high.

Once again, Bo Kimble was carrying the team with his scoring. We could win this game if we were patient and did not rush our shots. But patience was something we never practiced.

We had a 2-point lead with ten seconds remaining in the game. Alabama had one last chance and got the ball to their star, Robert Horry. Later in his NBA career, Horry would be known as Big Shot Rob, because of his clutch shooting in important games. In this game, Horry launched a jump shot as the clock ran down. It hit the rim, rolled around, and fell out. Watching the shot from our bench, it looked good, but luckily it was not. Nothing was going to stop the Lions. It wasn't time for Hank Gathers's team to lose. The run-and-gun Loyola Marymount team could even win slow, 62–60, over Alabama. If we could win slow, we could do anything.

We were in the Oakland arena watching the end of the UNLV game versus Ball State, which would determine whom we played next in the Elite Eight. It was a close game with two minutes remaining. Our players were actively cheering for UNLV to win. Clearly, the Running Rebels were the superior team, yet my team wanted to play UNLV in the next round. They wanted a crack at the Rebels for what happened to us way back in November.

We opened the season against UNLV in Las Vegas. Both teams boasted having a fast break offense with a tenacious full-court man-to-man defense. The UNLV coach, Jerry Tarkanian, prided himself in beating you up on defense and then running the ball down your throat. We showed up ready for that battle. Midway through the first half, we were up 10 points and clearly in charge of the game. We were too quick for the Rebels; we were relentless. They were breaking down. UNLV needed more than a time-out to fix the problem.

So they got a bomb scare.

The court officials announced the threat and asked everyone to stand up and look under their seats for a strange object, presumably a bomb. After ten thousand fans in the Thomas and Mack Center searched the building, the game was allowed to continue. Our players stayed on the bench for more than twenty minutes before resuming play. They were now flat and lethargic. Something finally slowed down our fast break—a bomb scare.

UNLV regained their poise, and our 10-point lead was cut to 2 by halftime. As both teams exited into the tunnel, there were words exchanged between their leaders Stacey Augmon and Larry Johnson and our stars Bo Kimble and Hank Gathers. The bomb scare had put everyone on edge. This was now more than a friendly contest. We regrouped at halftime and came out running the fast break and full-court press on defense. We were ready for twenty more minutes of the speed game. Put up or shut up. It was time to find out who could sustain this frantic pace. To our surprise, UNLV wanted none of it. They slowed the game down by playing a drop-back zone defense. They had had enough of the speed game; they were now playing the slow game.

Jerry Tarkanian's decision acknowledged that he wanted no part of running with us. He abandoned bragging rights in order to win the game. We were stuck in a slow game and were not prepared for it. With only a few weeks of practice before this first game, I did not practice against any zone defense. We were strictly run and shoot, run and shoot, no matter what. Jerry Tarkanian outsmarted me, and we struggled to score against their zone defense. We did not know how to handle the slow pace and lost to UNLV, 102–91.

After the game, Hank Gathers was beside himself with anger. He was angry we lost. He was angry with UNLV's players. He was angry with the bomb scare's delay. He was angry most of all with me. I had not prepared the team for a zone defense. I had embarrassed him in front of friends and family. In his eyes, I had failed him. After the game, in the locker room, Hank was so mad that he wouldn't even look at me. Hank was right. I failed. Jerry Tarkanian knew when to say, "Enough." I was so committed to the system that I refused to bend. It cost my team a win. Now, months later, at the end of the season, we had a chance to redeem ourselves against UNLV. That's why our players wanted the Rebels to beat the inferior Ball State. They wanted revenge. We were on a roll. We didn't care whom we played. Bring on the bad boys from Las Vegas. We should have beaten them on their home court; now we would show them in Oakland.

A major difference, however, was that we didn't have Hank Gathers, our fallen star. We had his memory. We had his spirit. But we didn't have his powerful, physical force. We didn't have his points and didn't have his rebounds. To beat UNLV, we needed Hank. I didn't have a good feeling as we entered the court to start the game. For the first time in the NCAA tournament, I felt the pressure to win, the pressure to continue our journey for Hank Gathers. All the good vibes of playing the game for fun went away. Now we needed to win to satisfy our growing fan base. People from all over the country had made us their team. We had to win for them. We could not disappoint the fans. But that is not what we set out to do. We had done it for love. We had done it for fun. We had done it for Hank.

Now, doing it for others entered into the equation. The weight of others was pulling us down. I was unhappy with the UNLV players individually coming down to our bench to shake hands and acknowledge our quest. I felt as if we were being invaded. The enemy was smashing our karma before the game even started. Both teams brought their run-and-gun style. UNLV was on their game. Their power forward, Larry Johnson, was unstoppable. We seemed off our game, as if distracted. After UNLV scored, we ran our fast break and threw the ball directly to their guard, who scored another basket. Instead of playing free and easy, without a care in the world, we played tense and confused, with the burden of the world on our shoulders. We made a run at their lead; but despite our efforts, it was not our day.

We lost, 131–101, and the dream was over. I was proud of our players, who performed so well, but felt relieved that it was over. We had won more than our ability. We were human; reality caught up with us. We had done enough for Hank. Now we had to live without him. Our team effort to honor Hank Gathers was over; now we had to honor him individually. This was a bigger challenge than winning games. Our playtime was over; our work time had just begun.

AFTER OUR FINAL game with UNLV, I was emotionally spinning around, trying to figure out what to do. I could stay at LMU and build on my fast break system, which had caught national attention, or I could leave and put behind me all the pain and sorrow surrounding Hank Gathers's death.

A new start would be a welcome change, yet my system was here with this team. LMU had made me a prominent coach; why should I abandon them? Out of nowhere, I got a call from Bernie Bickerstaff, the GM for the Denver Nuggets. He wanted to talk about their coaching position. During our meeting, Bernie was very direct. He told me they were prepared to offer me the job and would like an immediate answer. I said, "In two days, you will know."

This was my chance to get back into the NBA. I wanted to show the basketball world that I belonged and that I could win in this league. I knew the Nuggets were on a downward spiral, with key players retiring or being traded for future picks. This was not an ideal job, but for a two-time loser in the NBA—albeit with an NBA championship in my back pocket—this might have been my last chance as a head coach.

Cassie encouraged me to take the job even though this would be another move for our family. "Let's do it," she said.

After telling Bernie Bickerstaff we had an agreement, I went and told LMU's president, Father James Loughran, that I was leaving. Deep down I was not 100 percent certain I wanted to depart from LMU. I was looking for signs that this may be a mistake. Father Loughran showed no disappointment. He seemed relieved, as if my exit would bring closure to the explosion surrounding Hank's death. If I went, so would the memories of last season, both good and bad. I wouldn't say he pushed me out the door, but Father Loughran didn't try to stop me.

The next day, I flew to Denver to sign the contract. That night in the hotel, I again had second thoughts. I loved coaching the system at LMU, and I wanted to be a part of LMU's basketball future. I fell asleep thinking I would say no to Denver but woke up ready to coach the Nuggets. I would run my fast break system in the NBA, just as I had at LMU. I announced in the press conference, "My speed game is going to knock your socks off."

21

The Tipping Point

Coming directly from LMU and a successful experience with the system, I decided to implement the same running game in the NBA. The Nuggets were a struggling franchise losing most of their best players, such as Alex English, to retirement. It was time to build a new program.

I got a call from Dale Brown, LSU's coach, who wished me good luck and said that if I stayed at LMU, I was about to change the way basketball was played in college. He felt as though I was at the tipping point of other teams playing the speed game. I thanked Coach Brown for the compliment. The truth was that I really didn't want to leave LMU with the fast break system in place and the players committed to running it, but I felt as though it might be my last chance to coach in the NBA and I better not turn it down. The hope of the franchise was with the new players, especially our high-first-round pick, Chris Jackson, from LSU.

Chris was only a sophomore, but he was a prolific scorer in college. Chris became a holdout with contract negotiations spilling well into training camp. He arrived two days before our home opener, forty pounds overweight, and without his medication for his Tourette's syndrome. In short, Chris Jackson was a mess.

The players showed no sympathy for Chris. In the first practice, he was pushed around like a little boy who belonged in junior high rather than the

NBA. I soon realized that he was a misfit in my fast break system. He didn't have the speed to push the ball as a No. 1 guard or the size to be an effective No. 2 guard to catch and shoot. Chris Jackson was an out-of-shape tweener. The city of Denver hoped he was the answer; I saw his game as a problem.

After a few games, I asked Chris, if we were to run some ball screens for him, would that help his struggles on offense. He said, "No, I'm better with the ball, and get the defense away from me." In a five-man fast break system, this one-on-one style does not fit. Chris Jackson was in a system that didn't work for him, and our star draft choice didn't work for us.

Fortunately, we also had Michael Adams, who was the perfect point guard for my style. He had speed, and he could score. Michael took pride in making three-point shots. In our home opener, Michael was spectacular but couldn't finish the game with a pulled hamstring. He had been nursing his leg all preseason, and it returned to haunt him and us.

Don Nelson, the Golden State Warriors' coach, laughed at our simple offensive form. He read the *Denver Post* and saw a diagram of our fast break, and that was the entire scouting report for the game. It was a great game, with Golden State winning, 162–158. With Michael Adams healthy and fit for the entire game, we would have prevailed.

To bolster our young squad, we acquired two well-traveled veterans: Orlando Woolridge and Walter Davis. They had the experience, but not the legs, to help our youth. At the first practice, Davis came to me and said, "Coach, my legs are almost gone, so what do you want? Do you want me at practice or at games?" I said, "Walter, I want you at games." So Walter Davis never practiced and only played games. He was a talented shooter who made our fast break dangerous. Walter would go on streaks of eight, nine, ten jumpers in a row.

Before a game against the Lakers, Walter reminded me that Coach Dean Smith of North Carolina had a system where, if you were tired during a game, you put your fist up and he would take you out. After a rest, the player could go back in the game on his own volition. Well, Walter's condition now was such that when he came out of a game, his knees would lock up, and he couldn't run anymore that night. So in the Lakers game, Walter made seven straight jump shots and came down the court with his fist up.

I yelled out to him, "I'm not Dean Smith; you are not coming out of the game until you miss." Walter made four more shots and then missed. I subbed him out, and Walter Davis staggered to the bench, never to return.

In our first trip to Phoenix, Walter was especially animated to defeat the Suns. He had been a star with them for many years and now was returning to prove his worth. We were in a classic run-and-shoot game, with both teams scoring in eight seconds or less. Walter was scoring well against his former teammates, when he dove to save a ball from going out of bounds. He crashed into Jim Boyle, my assistant, who was frantically charting our shot attempts. Jim accidently stabbed Walter in the arm with his pen. Bleeding profusely, Walter went to the locker room with the score, 75–70, favoring Phoenix. Five minutes later Walter returned, bandaged up, and the score was 100–75. Walter went to Jim Boyle and said, "What happened?" I replied, "Jim stabbed you, and we went to hell without you. That's what happened."

At halftime, with the score 110–85, I went into the team room to encourage the players to keep running. Jim Boyle intercepted me and forced me into a little closet away from the team. He said, "We have a problem. They are going to score 200 points. I have a grandson who is watching this game in Philadelphia, and this is embarrassing." I responded, "I always wanted to be in a 200-point game." Jim barked, "But not the losing side!"

I assured Coach Boyle that Phoenix could not keep the pace to score 200 points. They would tire. So I had the team come back out and run the system. I felt confident that we wouldn't crack, and I hoped the Suns would. My prediction was correct; we only lost 173–143. A 200-point game was still out there.

I was convinced not only that my system would work in the NBA but that we would run the system and wipe out all the traditional ways of playing the pro game. In my first coaches' meeting before the start of training camp, I announced that we were going to full-court press on defense the entire forty-eight minutes. Consequently, we never had to practice half-court defensive situations.

The biggest defensive issue in the NBA was how to cover the ball screen. As the dribbler comes off a screen, some teams teach going over the screen, others go under the screen, others switch the screen, and others trap and double-team the screen. I solved the problem by not giving the opposition the chance to run a ball screen. We were playing full-court defense. The enemy would never get to a half-court ball screen situation.

Our press defense would lead to a wide-open game without all the half-court situations common to NBA basketball. The classic ball screen would be eliminated. My task was to get our players to aggressively defend the full court for the entire game. I soon found out that was not so simple.

Veteran players like Walter Davis and Orlando Woolridge refused to come up court to press; they wanted to fall back on defense and wait for the ball to start a traditional offense, featuring ball screens. We were teaching our players to come up aggressively and attack the ball in the full court; they were passively falling back and avoiding the problem. Both Orlando and Walter would tell me they "had my back." When the full-court press defense broke down, they would be there to cover the basket. But we needed them up the court to press and steal the ball; they refused and continued to fall back.

Without all five players pressing in the full court, we wound up playing more and more half-court defense, the very defense I purposely ignored to practice in training camp. My brilliant idea failed because I couldn't get the players to do it. No amount of practice was going to improve the defense. It was doomed.

We were stuck with no defense, so our only hope was that the fast break offense would save us. Running the ball as fast as we could on every possession for forty-eight minutes, we would wear out the opposition. We were better at offense. We were scoring at a league-leading pace; 120 points per game became routine for us.

Orlando Woolridge was leading the NBA in scoring. He came to us as a broken-down throwaway from the LA Lakers. He was too old to be effective for the Lakers; however, in the fast break system, Orlando found open shots he never could get in the slower half-court NBA style. The fast break system, ironically, made Orlando young again. The fast pace allowed him to drive the ball down the lane ahead of the defense. He smiled like a boy in a candy shop when everything was free for the taking. Orlando was outscoring Michael Jordan as we were piling up the points.

Unfortunately, Orlando got poked in the eye driving to the basket and sustained a torn retina. He was sidelined for a few weeks and returned with a full facial mask to protect the injured eye. He never returned to form. He was missing easy shots that were normally automatic. He told me the new goggles limited his vision and that he could barely see the basket. Without vision, the speed game was no advantage to Orlando Woolridge. He returned to being an old broken-down veteran.

With Orlando's demise, the fast break system sputtered. We got caught in more and more half-court situations, and we were not prepared for the half-court game, because my system teaches players to shoot the ball in five seconds and not to worry about the shot clock. It doesn't have plays to fall back on when the defense beats you down court. In the speed game, that won't happen. Way back in training camp, we needed the appearance of half-court offense to scrimmage. We had none, on purpose.

My assistant Jim Boyle said, "Give them my summer camp offense for kids." It was simple, directing the players to spread out and pass the ball five times and then shoot. There were no other rules. Because it was so simple, I liked the offense. Since it was our only play, we called it Denver. I was not pleased with passing the ball five times before taking a shot, so I altered it to Denver No. 1, which meant shooting on the first pass. Winning games became more and more of a challenge with a defense forced into half-court situations and an offense, minus the high-flying Orlando Woolridge, forced into set plays.

The fast break system needs a speedy point guard who can race the ball down the court ahead of the defense, but just as important is the outlet pass going to the guard. On made baskets by the opposition, the No. 5 man must outlet the ball to the point guard in a split second; otherwise, the fast break is over before it begins. The defense is back; now you must play "normal" five-on-five basketball.

Our starting center, Blair Rasmussen was very good at outletting the ball. He practiced diligently at taking the ball out of the net and passing to a streaking point guard thirty-five feet away. Blair was a lumbering big man who learned to play the speed game. He was a believer. Unfortunately, he threw the outlet pass so hard and so many times that he threw his shoulder out. It required surgery and ended Blair's outlet-passing career.

Our backup center was Greg "Cadillac" Anderson, who was eager to make the outlet pass to start our fast break. So eager, in fact, that frequently the ball would end up in the tenth row of the arena. Cadillac once said to me, "Coach, I'm going to kill someone in the loge section with my outlet pass." I responded, "Don't worry about accuracy; speed is more important."

I never yelled at a No. 5 man for misthrowing the pass. Sometimes I would chide the point guard for not catching it. The outlet pass was so important to the fast break that I was willing to absorb a few turnovers and fans with bloody noses.

My No. 5 man had to be freewheeling, not cautious. I was his biggest fan. During the off-season, I had Cadillac come to Denver from his home in Houston to drill the fast break. One of the drills was outlet passes off the wall, over and over, one hundred times. Greg Anderson was becoming an expert. There was a series of similar fast break drills I wanted him to do three times a week when he went back to Houston for the summer.

The final drill in the workout was to make five free throws in a row to end the session. If you missed a free throw, you had to dunk the ball five times and start over. Well, Cadillac had trouble making five straight free throws. He would make two and dunk five, make three and dunk five. Finally, after twenty attempts of five in a row, he did it. As we walked off the court, I put my arm around him with a smile of approval and said, "Just think, Cat, by the end of the summer you are going to be a great free-throw shooter." He said, "No, Coach, I'm going to be a great dunker." Greg Anderson was not the most talented basketball player, but he sure had the right spirit. He was a believer in the system. Five of him running the fast break could win.

My first season in Denver, we led the NBA in scoring, averaging 120 points per game. No one has averaged that many points since, including the 2015 NBA champion Golden State Warriors. Unfortunately, we gave up 130 points per game.

When we first met for training camp, Jim Boyle said that our old college coach, Jack Ramsay, had told him we'd win twenty games. I dismissed that prediction as far too low and focused on scoring points. We were going to knock your socks off.

Going into the last week of the season, we had nineteen wins, with two games remaining. One was at home against the Western Conference–leading San Antonio Spurs, and the other was at Houston. I said to Jim Boyle, "It looks like Jack Ramsay was wrong—we can't win twenty games." Boyle winked at me and said, "Coach Ramsay is always right."

That night, we beat the Spurs at home and knocked Larry Brown's San Antonio team out of first place. As we walked off the court, Jim Boyle gave me a knowing look and said, "I told you so."

The next season, we drafted Dikembe Mutombo from Georgetown University, a seven-foot-two shot-blocking defensive star with limited offensive skills. Like Chris Jackson, Dikembe was the future hope for the Nuggets.

The new president of operations, Tim Leiweke, promoted the team by announcing that season ticket holders could come to the opening home game and if they didn't like the product on the floor, they could get their season ticket money back. We lost the opener. I never heard how many fans requested their money back, but I knew my days were numbered. I had a friend from Philadelphia, George White, who was an administrative assistant with the Nuggets. George would occasionally go out with the coaches after a game for drinks. A few weeks into the season, George came to see me and said his superior advised him not to be seen with the coaches. It was not good for his career. The divide-and-conquer process had already begun.

Like Chris Jackson, Dikembe was not a great fit in my fast break system. Normally, the center takes the ball out of bounds on made baskets and then trails the break for an open eighteen-foot jump shot. Well, Dikembe couldn't get the ball out quickly, and for sure he couldn't make eighteen-foot jump shots. He could barely make lay-ups. I was getting heat from GM Bernie Bickerstaff to win or else, and I had a No. 5 man who couldn't play his part.

In desperation, I changed the positions in the fast break. For twenty years, the positions had always been the same, but because of Mutombo, they changed. I made Dikembe a No. 4 man whose role was to sprint down the court and run to our basket. No more jump shots. I was not pleased with myself for breaking up my fast break principle, but hopefully it would save Dikembe Mutombo and my job. To my surprise, Dikembe thrived in sprinting down the court. Night after night, he would beat the opponent's big man down the court and score an easy basket. Against the Boston Celtics he was scoring open lay-ups, as the great Robert Parish struggled to reach half court. Dikembe, the unskilled offensive player, averaged 19 points per game. Because he was willing to run as fast as he could, Dikembe Mutombo made his mark in a league full of talented offensive players. Even with Dikembe thriving more than ever expected, we didn't win enough games. The system worked for Dikembe but not for me. I was fired.

The first time I was fired, I took it personally. Clearly, it meant something was wrong with me. I was a failure. I didn't belong in the NBA. I was embarrassed to go home and face my wife and family. My kids came home from school crying because fellow students were laughing at them. In the world of the Los Angeles Lakers, Paul Westhead needed to vanish from the game and the fans.

All of this was just eighteen months after winning the NBA championship and Jerry Buss proclaiming that I was the brightest young coach in the world. The crash from greatness to unemployed was overwhelming. It took months for me, with the help of my wife, Cassie, and my four children, to rise up and want to start again in the coaching world.

Since my Lakers experience, I have been fired several times. After the first one, it becomes easier. You realize it's not personal; it's business. You were hired to win games, and if you don't win enough, you will be gone. Losing support from your team is more rapid when running the fast break. I promised speed, excitement, and winning. When the system failed to be full blast, it was slow, boring, and full of losses.

When I took the Denver Nuggets coaching position, I promised, "We are going to knock your socks off," with our speed game. Two years later the Nuggets asked me to leave town quickly, with or without my socks.

22

A Crazy Genius

All the world's a stage, and all the men and women merely players.
—WILLIAM SHAKESPEARE, *As You Like It*

In 2003 I was coaching the Long Beach Jam in the American Basketball Association (ABA). We were in Juarez, Mexico, for our opener, and I got a call from my agent, Warren Le Garie, who said, "I might have a job for you back in the real league, the NBA."

I said anything would be better than riding to the game in a farmworker's bus in Juarez.

Running the system, we played that night against the Juarez Matadors and won, 118–104. Matt Barnes, just out of UCLA, had made eight straight three-point shots to open up the contest. He never shot any threes in practice but, in the game, exploded from the outside.

That was to be Matt's first and last game in the ABA. He was picked up by the LA Clippers for the season. I also found out that there was a chance for me to go to the Orlando Magic. The team had fired Doc Rivers and made his assistant Johnny Davis their coach. Because Johnny Davis played for Jack Ramsay with the Portland Trailblazers, Davis thought I might be a fit.

The next day, I flew to Orlando for an interview. At dinner with Coach Davis, he said, "I hear from some people you are a genius, and I hear from others you are crazy. Which one is true?" I realized the answer would probably decide my fate, ABA or NBA. I answer that both were true: "I'm a crazy genius."

Johnny Davis smiled and said, "Can you start tomorrow?"

I soon found out that Johnny Davis wanted me to install the fast break with the Magic. Not easy to do midseason with veteran players who are losing. Our star was Tracy McGrady, who was a prolific scorer but who did not want to go fast or use any more energy than necessary. We couldn't get him to sprint on offense, and therefore, the others followed his lead.

The plain truth was that Tracy McGrady was the poster boy for offense at a moderate pace. When he was on his game, he could beat his defender and score at any time in any way; so why run fast? It was much easier to embrace the McGrady way than the Westhead way. The McGrady way was easy; my way was hard.

Because of McGrady, I allowed, for the first time, someone other than the point guard to bring the ball up on the fast break. My concession was that if Tracy got a defensive rebound, he could bring the ball up like a point guard and shoot or pass. McGrady was very good at this, but he only got a hand full of defensive rebounds. The rest of the offensive possessions were played at a normal steady-as-she-goes pace. The fast break didn't happen in Orlando that season.

Leading into training camp the following season, Coach Davis was more resolved to install my fast break. I had sold him on the system; the challenge was now to sell the players. Actually, in basketball, that is always the challenge, getting the players to buy in.

We had two new draft choices who the Magic believed were going to turn the team around. Dwight Howard, the six-foot-eleven athletic eighteen-year-old, was the first pick of the draft and was deemed to be the standard-bearer of the franchise.

For me, I saw a natural for my system. He could jump and touch the top of the backboard. With his long stride, he could run the full court in four seconds. There was only one problem: Dwight Howard was not at all interested in the running game.

He fell right in line with the NBA way of taking his time getting to the offensive end. Dwight turned a deaf ear to the speed game. In the beginning of the season, I gave him the benefit of his inexperience, as to why he wasn't running hard every time on offense. I had an assistant trainer chart every offensive possession of Dwight on how hard he ran. A simple 1–10 chart with 10 being the fastest. Game after game, the chart would be full of 3s, 4s, and 5s, rather than 8s, 9s, or 10s.

I would show this to Dwight, but he did not change his pace. Like many NBA players, Dwight Howard saw the transition time from defense to offense as the chance to catch your breath before going to work. The system preaches the opposite. Sprint when others are taking their time.

I thought that additional work might lead to Dwight buying in, so when fellow assistant Clifford Ray had to leave early one day and asked me to work with Dwight after practice, I said yes. I gave him twenty low-post moves to catch my pass and score. On each occasion, Dwight was totally disinterested in making the correct move to score.

At the end of twenty attempts, I stopped, walked over to Dwight, and said, "This is the worst workout I have ever had with a player." I turned and walked away.

I should have tried something else. I should have asked, "What's wrong; are you okay?" But I didn't. I felt insulted by his lack of effort.

I left the arena thinking we would never see Dwight Howard become a superstar. Deep down he was not willing to work hard enough to make it happen. Of course, he would end up lasting a lot longer in Orlando than I did.

OUR SECOND DRAFT choice was Jameer Nelson, the highly regarded point guard from St. Joseph's. Jameer had all the tools to be the perfect speed guard for the fast break. I immediately befriended him as a fellow St. Joe's Hawk and told him he was going to lead us to the promised land. With him, we were going to lead the NBA in scoring. I told him to take the ball, push it at breakneck speed, and pass to the open teammates for baskets.

Early on, in practice and into games, Jameer did not take the bait. I went to Johnny Davis and said, "We have a problem." Coach Davis listened and said, "Well, Paul, what are you going to do about it?" That was a stroke of genius by Johnny Davis. Since I found the problem, I was in charge of solving it.

I worked every day in practice to get Jameer to speed dribble the ball. I broke down game video and showed him his offensive possessions, some very fast but many at half speed with way too many dribbles. Jameer knew exactly what I wanted but refused to get caught up in a running game. I finally figured out why. If he ran the ball down court in three seconds and passed, his role as an NBA point guard would be diminished. Jameer wanted to display his craft to the NBA—how to run plays, how to get his team into offensive sets, how to read the defense and direct his teammates. He realized that all this goes away if you speed dribble and pass for scores ahead of the defense.

He was right. His career in the NBA was better served by playing slower. Unfortunately, without a push guard, the system was doomed. We lost too many games with a slower pace. Midseason, Johnny Davis was fired. I had failed to deliver the fast break.

AFTER MY LMU coaching experience, I searched the world, literally, to find a team that would run the system. I went back into the NBA with professional players but came up short with the Denver Nuggets.

I went back to college basketball at George Mason University, in Virginia, attempting to produce the system with a new version called Paul Ball. We trained on the track with parachutes attached to our players' backs, sprinting into the wind, creating a drag on my players. Their speed increased, but their desire to play fast the entire game never caught on. We could beat our opponents on the track but not on the basketball court.

My coaching life was spinning around looking for a team to press and run, and I looked anywhere, including Japan, where I coached the Panasonic Super Kangaroos, who, of all teams besides LMU, embraced my system most of all.

Still, ultimately, each time, the speed game failed, and each time, I was run out of town.

I then took a job coaching women's basketball with the Phoenix Mercury in the WNBA. Before arriving in Phoenix, I worked out Diana Taurasi in Los Angeles. I needed to find out what position in the system she could play.

We tried her at No. 1, pushing the ball a hundred miles per hour, and she couldn't keep up. We tried her at No. 3, running the left side full speed over and over every possession, and she couldn't keep up. We invited her back the next day to try other positions, but she was a no show, never to call back or return for further evaluation. So my best player on the Mercury, and the best women's player in the world, was not fit for the system. Visions of Dwight Howard danced in my head.

However, when I arrived in Phoenix, Dee Taurasi met me at the airport to drive together to sign the contract. This was the only time a player came to meet me to start a coaching position. She said, "Treat us like the guys; don't water down your system."

I gave them the complete dose of full-court press defense and fast break offense. They couldn't do it. We were losing games. But it wasn't the fast break that broke them; it was the full-court defense. The combination of defense and offense was too much. Eventually, I backed off the full-court defense and had them play more half-court zone.

By midseason we were playing well. We started the season at 2-7, and I said to myself, "Oh no, here comes another failure." Most teams, when the fast break doesn't work early on, give it up, because it's so hard. The WNBA women did not give up on the break. They kept trying to run the system as I designed it. We won our last seven games of the season and were the best in the league. Unfortunately, we got off to such a slow start that we were in a four-way tie for the last playoff spot, and we were left out of the playoffs because of secondary qualifications. We were the best team with nowhere to go. Our players said, "Let's go on the road and play anybody." Now the system was in their blood; the next season would show the world fast break basketball.

In my second season with the Mercury, our fast break was on a roll. On the road in Houston, Diana Taurasi had scored 47 points with four minutes remaining in the game. I ran a set play for her, and she passed. I ran another play for her, and again she passed. I said, "Dee, you need 2 points to break the scoring record." Taurasi responded, "Coach, I had enough for tonight; let Jen Lacy get some points."

Diana Taurasi is the best women's basketball player in the world. She has the talent and toughness to overcome any opponent. However, she was not a good fit for my fast break system. She wouldn't explode and run at full speed. Dee wanted to pace herself. Like all gifted athletes, Dee knew her optimal speed.

Fortunately, we had acquired a guard from Indiana, Kelly Miller, who turned out to be the perfect point guard for the fast break. Some players embrace the system instantaneously, as if they were born to run. In our first practice, I told Kelly Miller, "I want you to push the ball as fast as you can, and do it forever."

For the next two years, in every practice and game, Kelly Miller pushed the ball at breakneck speed, every possession. She helped ignite the talented Taurasi to run along with her. Kelly Miller was the perfect player to make Dee go faster. Once Dee Taurasi received the ball down court, she scored at will. The lead dog, Kelly Miller, pushed the star, Taurasi, to greatness.

There were games when Kelly struggled emotionally. Opponents knew she was sensitive and jeered at her, "Why don't you cry, you little baby?" Kelly did not take this well at all. On one of these occasions, Kelly was breaking down emotionally, and another player, Cappie Pondexter, came over to her and said, "If they say another thing to you, I'm going to kick their ass." Kelly got right back into our speed game. Cappie had her back.

Despite the constant speed of our point guard, there were times when Dee didn't sprint out on offense. One trick I used to push her was to let her lead the break. Whenever Diana got a defensive rebound, she was given the green light to be the point guard for that possession. So for five to ten times a game, Dee was the lead guard, pushing the ball and making plays at a fast pace.

In small doses, Dee was great at running the system. For most of the game, Dee was a No. 2 guard who ran down the court ahead of the ball to shoot open shots. When she did this, Diana was unstoppable. Jump shots and drives to the basket were easy pickings for her. When she didn't sprint full speed down the court, she trailed the ball at her own pace. To my displeasure, Dee would nonetheless receive the ball late in the break. The team knew she was the best and would accommodate her misgivings in the speed game. Many times, however, the trail position worked to her advantage, because the defense got back waiting for her. She caught the pass open and scored an easy wide-open jump shot. Sometimes, players know more than their coaches. The fast break system says to sprint every possession; the superstar says, once in a while, I know better.

WE MADE IT to the WNBA finals against the defending champion, the Detroit Shock. It went to the fifth and deciding game in Detroit. No team had ever won the championship on the road.

During my pregame talk in the locker room, Cappie Pondexter had a question: "What's with your shoes, Coach? They don't match. One has a tassel, and the other doesn't." I responded, "I'm just a poor kid from Philadelphia, and that's how we dress." The team all laughed and went out ready to run the system. We immediately took a 15-point lead and never looked back.

We beat Detroit on the road and won the WNBA championship. As a coach, it took me twenty-seven years to win another title since the Los Angeles Lakers. I felt as though the fast break would triumph again, but I never thought it would take so long. When the team commits to the speed game, we win. When the players embrace the fast break, it is the best way to play the game of basketball.

So why do it?

Why run my system and take the chance to look bad, to lose games, to be insulted, and ultimately get fired?

I guess I could say that when the run-and-gun system works, it's the best. It's alive, it's free, it's fulfillment. I am not sure basketball will ever see this style of play again. There are too many factors holding the speed game back. An occasional glimpse of fast break basketball, like the Stephen Curry–led Golden State Warriors, is not the system. The Warriors are one of the best teams in all basketball but make no attempt to press and run. They make no attempt to run the speed game for the entire game. So if the best have ignored my style, why would anyone try it? Press and run nonstop is simply too hard to sustain. It's too demanding on coaches and players and too much of a commitment to find out what's waiting for you if you do it. Remember, you have to be a little crazy to try the speed game and totally out of your mind to stick with it.

So why do it?

My fast break system was very difficult. Failure was frequent, but every once in a while it worked. My Loyola Marymount team was a joy to coach. Players blended their talents together and performed to perfection.

In his book *Born to Run*, Bruce Springsteen talks about putting a rock band together and describes it as a trick involving chemistry, luck, and quicksilver, something that can produce a moment that lasts a lifetime. "When the world is at its best," he writes, "when we are at our best, when life feels fullest, one and one equals three."

Perhaps that doesn't sound logical, but then, I was never a big fan of logic. That's why, I suppose, I never had a plan B. After being fired by the Nuggets, I was back home saying goodbye to my youngest daughter, Juliet, who was flying to Denver to start college at the University of Colorado. Even though I had been run out of town, Juliet was welcome. She made the cut.

Because I was a committed fast break coach, I frequently was out of work and looking for a new gig where I could teach the speed game. Since my teams scored high numbers, there was always interest in my scheme. I interviewed for the coaching position at Tulane.

Cassie and I were invited to the campus for two days. We met school officials, had dinner with alumni groups, and felt as though we were going to be offered the basketball job. After a whirlwind tour of New Orleans and the campus, they asked me to stay another day. They would come to my hotel and announce the decision. We waited all day in our hotel room until an assistant athletic director came and said, "Thank you for your interest, but we have selected someone else."

I then realized Tulane had two candidates in town at the same time so that if one didn't work out or said no, they would pick the other. I felt all along as though I was their man, but I was their backup man. In another hotel was my coaching friend Roy Danforth, who was selected as Tulane's new coach.

Sometimes you don't get that close to a job. I once applied for a coaching position with the Air Force Academy, and after a few weeks I received a letter saying, "Thank you for your interest, but we have narrowed our field to twenty top coaches, and you did not make the cut." Losing out to the talented Roy Danforth was one thing, but losing to twenty coaches more qualified than you, that hurts.

In light of those crashes and burns, Cassie gave me some heartfelt advice.

"Tell them you are going to be like a normal coach," she said. "It's okay to run some fast break, but not every possession, every game. Paul, that's what gets you fired. Now we have to move again and look for another job."

"Normal. Hmmm, I can do normal," I thought.

Sure enough, I got a call from Jack Kvancz, the athletic director at George Mason University. He had some interest in my coaching background as a college and NBA coach. Jack wanted to meet and find out who I really was and what I would bring to their basketball team.

As I flew to Dallas for the crucial job interview, I was keenly aware of Cassie's advice: be "normal."

I knew she meant well. I knew she was tired of packing up and moving the family to another city. I knew the speed-game approach got me fired, but my fast break would also get me hired. There was always a team that wanted to play fast, and I was the guy to do that for you. I met with Jack Kvancz and discussed my coaching philosophy. He seemed interested and said, "Why should George Mason University hire you as our basketball coach?"

I thought of Cassie, her prudent counsel, her pleas to be normal. I then looked Jack Kvancz dead in the eye and said, "With my fast break system, I'm going to knock your socks off!"